The Art of Flowering Bonsai

The Art of Flowering Bonsai

PETER D. ADAMS

PHOTOGRAPHS BY BILL JORDAN

WARD LOCK

*This book is dedicated
to the memory of my fellow
artist, Christian Caspar*

A WARD LOCK BOOK

First published in the UK 1998 by Ward Lock
Wellington House 125 Strand
London WC2R 0BB

A Cassell Imprint

Distributed in the United States
by Sterling Publishing Co., Inc.
387 Park Avenue South, New York, NY 10016-8810

Distributed in Canada
by Cavendish Books Inc.
Unit 5, 801 West 1st Street
North Vancouver, B.C., Canada V7P 1PH

A British Library Cataloguing in Publication Data block for this book may be
obtained from the British Library

ISBN 0-7063-7625-0

Designed and typeset by Peter Butler
Printed and bound by Colorcraft Ltd., Hong Kong

Contents

Preface

When I was asked to write this book, it occurred to me that this is number seven! Writing seven books on anything suggests an obsession, and I thought back to when I was at art school and first got the fever. I can still remember that tree: a prostrate juniper that I potted into a plastic bowl my mother used for hyacinths. I bought, potted, wired and trimmed it in a single session – it took seven hours – and went to bed at two o'clock in the morning, having discovered what I really wanted to do with all that art training. Amazingly the tree lived and I was hooked.

I have now lived with bonsai for over forty years, and this is still the one art form I have never signed off and walked away from. The renewed freshness, fascination and charm pull me now and next year and…. Tending a tree every day is a process that allows the grower to add some personal element to its beauty. Working like this with plants in an era when people have little to do with the organic and the real provides an ultimate therapy and return of peace of mind.

A good bonsai makes you feel as if you have seen its image somewhere. It is the art behind art, when a tiny tree, maybe less than 60cm (2ft) high, can give you the feeling of time and place. Although it is the product of many interlinked techniques, a bonsai should look as if it has never been touched by a human. It should be entirely natural and make you feel that every element of it is almost inevitable.

Flowering bonsai can make a great impact. For most people there is something magical about the seasons enjoyed through a bonsai that bears flowers and berries. There is a familiar warmth and friendly association here that other plants simply do not have. Flowering trees have not had a bad press as much as no press at all, yet they make excellent bonsai, and for the most part they are easy to grow.

The book gives a mix of basics, sources, horticultural support, artistic evaluation and the fun of 're-creation', when trees are discussed and explained. However you use it, whether to help you create your own designs or just to browse through, I hope you enjoy it and wish you every enjoyment and success with your flowering bonsai.

I should like to thank my wife Kate for her unfailing support and many hours of practical help with this project and my old friend Bill Jordan for his wonderful photographs and for the time and travelling he put in for me and for all his support.

I should also like to thank the following people for their help in letting Bill and I photograph and display their flowering bonsai in the book: Mike Andrews, Malcolm and Kath Hughes, John Lee, Colin Lewis, Ian McLean, Ken Norman, Cordelia Silva and Mike Valentine.

P.D.A.

Introduction

What is a bonsai? Bonsai are trees grown in a container and kept small by a mixture of dwarfing techniques. Humans have carefully studied and adapted each of these techniques from nature.

Natural Dwarfing Factors

High Altitude Exposure to extreme levels of ultraviolet radiation at high altitudes will keep plant growth compact.

Weather Constant winds often sculpt trees into wind-blown patterns. The weight of snow buckles and twists trunks. Frost affects growth not covered by snow, killing it back to the protective coating and keeping the tree small. Drought causes die-back and changes in lateral shape or incredibly slow growth.

Limited Soil Compact root growth occurs when the roots are confined by heavy subsoil or in a rock pocket or crevice, often with the additional factors of extreme porosity or of drowning in trapped water.

Damage Trees fall on other trees causing die-back. Earthquakes and rock slides cause trunk realignment and will twist and distort normal growth. Hungry animals will prune new shoots mechanically every year.

Dwarfing Factors Adapted from Nature

High Altitude By placing bonsai in sunlight, the shortening effects of ultraviolet rays on plant growth can be used, but too much drying sun can cause die-back. The foliage colour of exposed trees is yellow. Growers use dappled shade to keep trees well lit but happily damp and blue-green.

Weather Good air circulation 'exercises' the tree, encouraging it to make stronger roots in response to the minimal movement of the trunk, and this has a slight dwarfing effect. Leaf disorders and bugs are also discouraged by air movement. The trick is the degree of wind exposure: once in a pot, the tree has only pot moisture available to it and once that drops, too much wind desiccates the tree. The other weather extremes described are avoided. Once it has been potted, a tree's tolerance is totally changed.

Limited Soil Plants growing in sandy soil in nature prove to have wonderful, fibrous roots, and many bonsai prosper in similar soil. Flowering trees often require a mixture of organic components, but this should still drain well. Wisteria is the exception, preferring a heavy type of soil.

Container This is both flowerpot and picture frame. It should be big enough to accept the roots and to act as a perfectly draining reservoir. Combined with the factor of limited soil, it acts like the rock crevice in containing growth.

Potting, Repotting and Root Pruning Roots are periodically pruned to keep the plant happily growing inside the small container. The lower, heavier parts of the root system are removed to promote the growth of lively feeder roots. Surface roots springing from the base of the trunk add age and character to the trunk and are retained.

Pruning and Wiring This is the counterpart of natural damage. Top growth is trimmed to create compact limbs and foliage, to give characterful changes of growth direction, to maintain a balance with the roots and to admit light and air to crowded parts of the tree. Most trees have apical dominance, and this means the upper portions need careful pruning to retain and build taper. Exceptions are azaleas and to some extent quinces, which are basally active. Wiring adds form and grace to the branches and twigs.

Watering Adequate water is a key element in plant health and in maintaining flower and fruit production. Constant dampness is better than flooding and drought.

Feeding This varies with the species, and there are guidelines for each in the section on Seasonal Care.

PART I

How Bonsai are Created

THE PRINCIPLES THAT FOLLOW
ARE BASED ON OBSERVATIONS OF
NATURAL DWARFING.

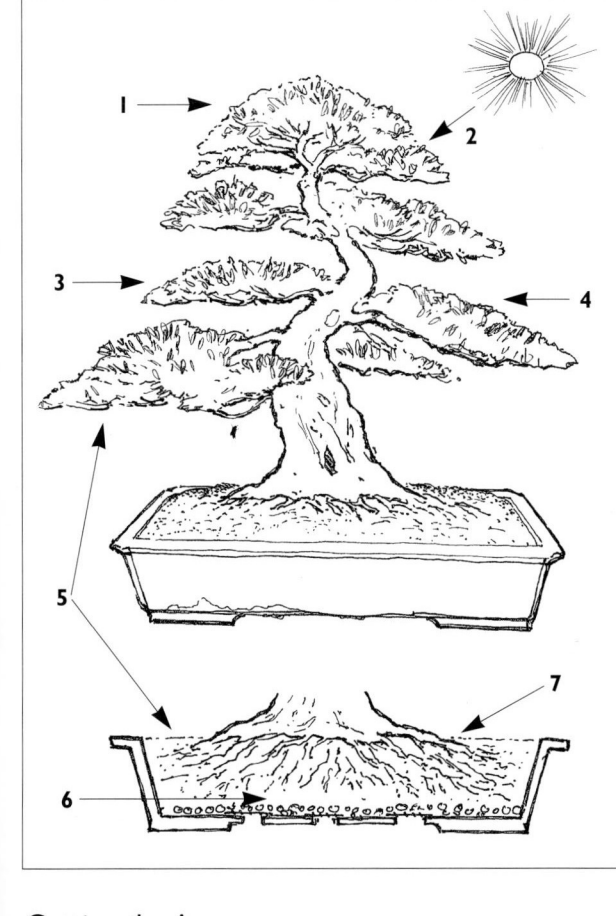

Main Principles

1 Cutting the natural apex redirects growth energy, diffusing it through the plant. Upper trunk branching is kept thinned and small. Lower limbs are allowed to become full and are, therefore, heavier. The wood fattens according to the burden of foliage it carries.

2 Position in full sun is a dwarfing factor. Ultraviolet light tidies foliage texture. Thinning allows the sun to reach inside branches and keeps the whole tree happy.

3 Pruning creates finer foliage texture because growth multiplies and diffuses growth energy. It also channels energy. Wiring adds a graceful shape.

4 Thinning increases ventilation and discourages pests. Air movement slightly rocking the trunk also dwarfs growth.

5 Root and branch mirror each other. If the top growth is fine, so is the root growth. If the roots are damaged, top growth is meager.

6 The soil must drain well. Regular watering to maintain even dampness is vital.

7 Root pruning rejuvenates the root system and the tree, allowing it to live in a happy and slow growing manner.

8 Feeding and pest control are vital.

Cutting the Apex

Cutting the apex is a fundamental step that limits height and redirects growth down through the plant. It is what happens when you trim a hedge. Growth is neatened and energy sent back down the system to keep the lower areas vigorous. The lower trunk/branch areas swell as the energy pumps through and reinforces the desired taper in the trunk. If apical pruning is not periodically repeated, the plant grows away and taper is lost. The trunks of badly overgrown bonsai sometimes revert to a columnar form.

The trunk is the sculptural core of the design. It should taper and have rough or smooth bark according to the aged appearance of the species. The shape decides the form of the branches, roots and container. The angle or posture should work well with the structure of the pot.

Cutting the apex redirects the plant's vigour.

Roots and Root Pruning

The roots of a bonsai are pruned so that the tree can live comfortably inside a small container. Pruning the older, lower roots promotes the growth of fine feeder roots and also creates a positive implosion of energy in the tree by reversing the ageing process. In nature old trees lose the energy to transfer food completely from the extended root circle, collapse and die back. Root pruning slows growth through division of energy but gives the bonsai a boost by moving all the vital feeder roots back under the trunk.

The older, upper roots are not pruned but are placed radially on the surface so that they splay out over the soil, steadying the tree in the pot. From artistic and practical points of view their eroded pattern can suggest great age and adds a solid and believable buttress to the trunk. The main roots should flow naturally into the soil with no minor roots crossing any major ones to diminish the sense of scale.

Old trees lose the energy to transfer nutrition from the extended root circle.

Repotting. The roots are washed.

Root pruning keeps feeder roots active close to the trunk.

Older roots are trimmed back, and the roots are reduced by about a third.

The trimmed root mass.

A mirror is created above and below the soil: fine roots correspond to fine branches.

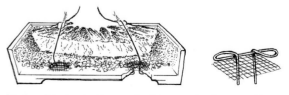

Section showing potting up. Drainage netting is secured in place with a 'butterfly' of shaped wire. Tie wires are passed through the drainage holes. A drainage course is added, then soil mix. The tree is positioned on the soil, tied in and more soil is added, making sure there are no air pockets, the surface is levelled and the plant watered in.

Butterfly, drainage netting, drainage course and main soil.

Branches and Branch Pruning

Like the trunk, branches are pruned to keep them in scale and to preserve and create taper, that all-important factor indicating age. Unpruned branches lack taper and look as if they grew in a year. An older appearance is achieved in a number of ways, the chief of which being the periodic replacement of the terminals by pruning, sometimes deeply, and replacing the extended branch line by wiring a side branch into position. This creates stepped taper, a desirable change of direction indicating age, and shortens the branch keeping the shape compact.

Branch terminals are pruned.

Re-growth is wired into position.

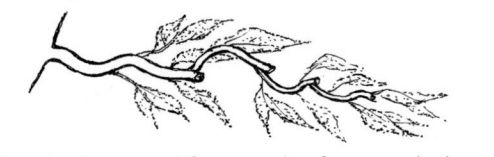

When this is repeated for a couple of seasons, the branch takes on taper.

Carefully shaped branches, combined sympathetically with the trunk, express structural form as a sculptor might. They give additional motion to the tree and unify the form through the contours of their repeated motif. Although similar, they should vary to add interest and avoid a mechanical look. The most convincing branches change direction more than once, have sharp angles as well as curves and taper towards their terminals. Twig loading is

Branches and trunk work together.

Branches are simplified by pruning and developed.

The sculptural core, showing angles working together.

Branches are trained to form contoured structures.

Structures are thinned and refined with wiring.

The untrimmed tree form.

The trimmed tree form.

minimal near the trunk and gains density towards branch ends. Branches are also pruned to suit the trunk form by creating negative areas or by building contours and creating an 'armature' for the finer side branches that make up the profile.

Leaves, Fruit and Flowers

Leaves work with the branches and trunk to complete the picture of the diminutive tree. Leaf weight, or density, makes wood. The tree expands according to the work it does, and leaf thinning gives the grower some control over wood thickening. Leaves are, therefore, important to the dwarfing process as well as being pretty, and thinning them does more than just make a less shrubby shape. It also admits light and air and keeps the interior parts of the tree perky, while the movement of air discourages bugs. The pruned profile fine tunes the branch form.

Lower lines are cleaned of hanging leaves.

The fruit and flowers cannot be reduced in size, and to keep a believable scale those trees that bear smaller fruit and flowers are preferred for bonsai. There is a huge choice, and I have tried to suggest suitable varieties.

Wiring

When it is used with good pruning schedules, wire shaping controls the form minutely. Wiring adds graceful bends to otherwise youthful and straight

The branches are first trimmed back to the contour line.

growth. As soon as the branch bends a little the line is aged.

The metal used is aluminium or copper. Anodized aluminium wire made for bonsai is soft and gentle to the tree. Copper hardens and conducts temperature rather too well, heating up in the summer and icing up in the frost. Aluminium is the wire to use for flowering plants, most of which have sensitive bark.

In applying wire to the tree, try to be neat and use consistent spacing between the coils. Coil angles at 45 degrees are standard. Do not use wire that is too thick or too thin for the job. If the wood is thin, wire that is too thick causes it to buckle in and out of the coils. Wire that is too thin for the job is maddening when it will not hold the bend. Test the resistance of the designated tree area and then the wire by bending them slowly. If the resistance feels about equal, you probably have the right gauge. Remember as you progress along the branch, as the wood tapers, that your wire should drop in thickness to avoid crushing the wood.

The 'finger clamp' supporting and bending.

How not to bend. There is a great risk of breaking.

After shaping.

The viewing side.

Side view showing apex coming forward.

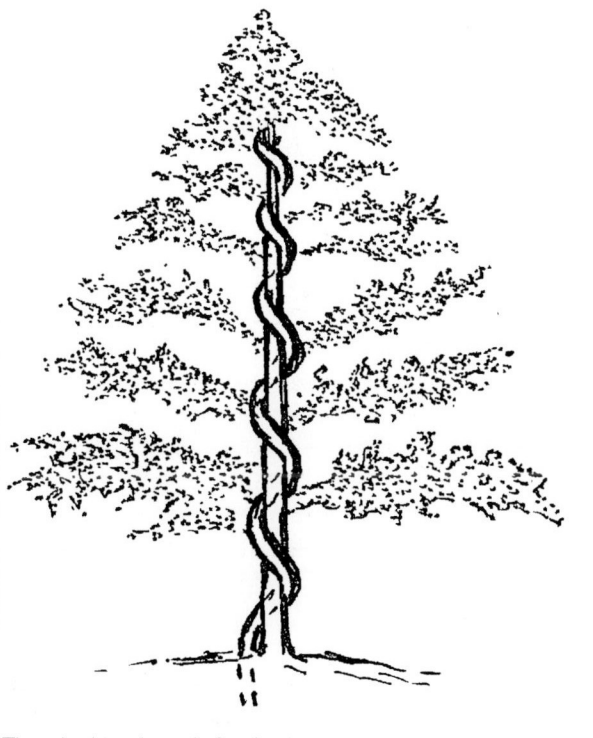

The wired trunk ready for shaping.

Cut the wire so that it is long enough to anchor firmly – wiring is all about leverage. Branches are best wired by going from one branch, around the trunk, to another branch. Trunks are wired from the base, starting by burying the wire in the soil as an anchor and beginning at the back of the trunk (check the diagrams for details).

The leverage principle in wiring is made more effective with even coiling. Place the coils closer at bends to give greater control, and try not to cross wires as you go along. Overlaps of wire at terminals can be neatly looped back. Do not leave wires sticking out.

Leverage is used to straighten and bend trunks, to suspend or pull down branches and even to make trunk 'templates', which are metal pieces in the desired shape to which the trunk is strapped. Whatever the method, from the lightest wire to the heaviest clamp, always use the minimum pressure on the wood. Do not crush it or you will get die-back. Protect leverage points with foam rubber or wrap them with raffia.

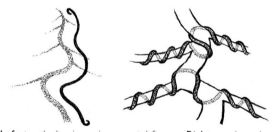

Left: trunk shaping using a metal former. **Right:** passing wire round the trunk maximizes leverage from branch to branch.

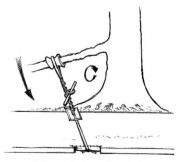

A wire is passed through the soil and the drainage hole and looped over the pot wall and branch. Friction points are cushioned and then a turn-buckle is used to twist and shorten the loop. This lowers the branch to the desired angle.

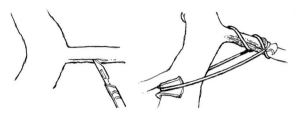

Left: the bark of a stubborn branch is first scored.
Right: the branch is then pulled down and the wound tissue makes the branch rigid.

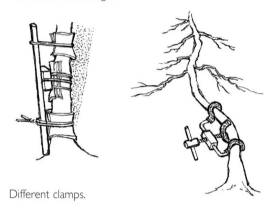

Different clamps.

Heavy branches that have a decided mind of their own can be made to hold the wired line by making a slit in the bark along and beneath the branch. As the bark heals, it forms a double callus and this effectively stiffens that area and the wiring holds. If you change your mind later on, of course, you have twice as much trouble!

Very heavy branches that will not bend are partly hollowed out beneath and wires are put into the recess. These lateral wires and the entire branch are wire coiled, and the whole area can then be bent without undue straining.

Hollowing a branch and laying wire in the recess allow big branches to be bent freely.

The technique for bending brittle wood is to apply the wire and clamp your hands around the area, making sure you overlap the fingers. Make a fist, pressing the area firmly so every part is supported, and squeeze and bend simultaneously. The wood will not break.

If your wiring is not a hundred per cent successful at first, keep working at it. It is better to create a design than to forget it in the effort of applying 'good' wiring!

Feeding

Feeding enables the tree to live happily inside the micro-environment of the container. Most flowering bonsai are grown for their seasonal appeal, and if they are to bear the best possible crop of flowers and fruit, they need phosphorus and potassium. The feed that is most effective is one that contains nitrogen, phosphorus and potassium in the proportions 0–10–10 – that is, no nitrogen.

In spring it is a good thing to give the tree a little nitrogen to perk it up a bit and to colour the foliage. A feed like Miracle-Gro at half strength will green up foliage nicely. Miracid at half strength is good for those plants, such as azaleas, that prefer acid soil.

During the season to maintain leaf colour without encouraging growth, which interferes with the flower/fruiting cycle, use some fish emulsion. This is really a background feed that will not push growth.

All plants need an annual 'fix' of trace elements. The easiest way to supply this is as a powder, such as Trace Element Frit, which supplies iron, manganese, zinc, boron, copper and molybdenum. Plants are given half a teaspoonful in spring. Fast-grown developing bonsai are fed with full-strength fertilizer. Miracid and Miracle-Gro are both good. Use 0–10–10 from midsummer to harden growth.

Detailed feeding advice for each plant is included under Seasonal Care.

Watering

Keep plants damp, particularly before feeding. If watering is too generous, sappy growth is produced. If water is withdrawn plants wilt. Somewhere in the middle lies 'damp'. You must find that point and make it work for you, because every location is different. Shaded plants need less water.

Most trees appreciate having the foliage sprinkled in the evening, but do not spray the flowers. During the day try to avoid hitting the leaves if you have to water in hot conditions. There is a possibility of leaf damage in direct sun, although this will be minimal.

Take it easy in the interval between watering applications with newly potted or repotted trees, because they need time to repair root damage before they can handle routine watering. Shade the tree and spray the leaves to supplement the moisture balance in the plant. Watch winter watering: aim for 'light' dampness. If frost is likely and your trees must be watered, do it early in the day. I always place my trees under the growing benches and surround them with heavy, clear polythene curtains. In cold weather this stops the wind freeze-drying and desiccating the foliage/top of the tree while the roots are incapable of transferring water.

As you gain expertise with your watering can or hose or whatever you use, you will gradually realize how your plant grows. I mean that literally: every plant is different, with different requirements, almost a personality. When you can look at your plant and know if it is damp, you understand watering.

Bonsai Potting Soil

There is a great deal of information available on potting soils now, a lot of it in the form of recipes from far away. I found out the hard way that plants must be grown with regard to local conditions and with an understanding of simple, basic composts.

When I began importing trees in the 1960s, I noticed that those with the best roots were grown in a river sand mix. Not only the roots, but every part of these trees was brimming with health. I remembered having read something advocating high sand content in potting soils. Here was proof!

The river sand was composed of rounded and angular sand, and it induced masses of roots when it was mixed with light organic material.

Sand Combine medium aquarium gravel with a potting grit or chicken grit. This will give a sand that has angular and rounded particles. Sieve the dry sand to remove any granules finer than 0.5mm (¹⁄₆₄ in) in size. Aim for a mix of between half-pinhead- to matchhead-size granules, a size that is based on the observed texture of river sand.

Peat Compost and Soil-less Compost There are a number of these compounds, such as erica-ceous mix and New Horizon, which are fibrous in texture. Fir bark would probably have similar texture.

Leaf Mould Composted oak and beech leaves are best.

Akadama This granular subsoil is imported from Japan. Check your source carefully to ensure that it is not recycled stuff that will soon break down, losing the desirable granular texture. Akadama will retain moisture, so the inclusion of a small quantity can be useful for thirsty species. It can clog easily if it has been already used, so do not use too high a percentage in your mix. Keep trees in akadama free of frost.

Quince and wisteria prefer a heavier soil. Wisteria needs a heavy and restricted root situation if it is to flower freely, a typical stress syndrome. Pomegranate trees also flower well with 'tight feet'.

I have included some soil recipes based on growing bonsai in the western hemisphere in Seasonal Care. I hope they will work for you.

Tools

There are tools for every conceivable job in bonsai. Whether they are necessary is highly debatable. A lot of tools are there for show or for that once-every-twenty-year job. You can do admirably with a few good basic tools.

Japanese flowering quince 'Chojubai'.

- **Trimming shears,** 15–20cm (6–8in) long, are used for root pruning.
- **Long-handled trimming shears,** 20–23cm (8–9in)long, are used for getting between twigs and branches.
- **Fine scissors,** 13–15cm (5–6in) long, are used for detailing branches and foliage.
- **Wire cutters,** 20–23cm (8–9in) long are built with excellent leverage, and their cutting action makes de-wiring easy.
- **Branch cutters,** 20–23cm (8–9in) and more long, are like pincers but with slanted blades and are used for branch removal. They make precise cuts and are kind to plant tissue, which heals well.
- **Jin pliers,** 20–23cm (8–9in) long, are used for bark stripping when making decorative areas out of redundant branch tissue. Also useful for turning over ends when finishing off wiring.
- **Rake** for combing out roots.
- **Anodized aluminium training wire,** in 1–6mm ($^1/_{32}$–$^1/_4$) gauges. You need the softness of this wire if you are working with flowering trees.
- **Turntable** is invaluable for assessing your tree as you work. Bonsai are very three-dimensional, and the turntable helps you to appreciate each facet of the shape.
- **Soil sieve** with 0.5–6mm ($^1/_{64}$–$^1/_4$in) mesh screens. Get a good one.
- **Trunk/branch splitter** consists of elongated pincers with wide jaws. They enable you to work on large diameter wood and can be used to slice away heavy roots.
- **Saw** made for the job saves temper when removing big branches.
- **Larger wire cutters.**
- **Root cutters,** large pincers with wide jaws, make precise cuts. Often used on azaleas.
- **Fine-nosed branch cutters** are used in detailing sub-branches and thicker twigs.
- **Jacks** in various patterns and sizes are used for easing shapes or modifying the angles of wired areas.
- **Short-handled chisels and knives** are useful for shaping, detailing and finishing jin.
- **Paintbrushes** are used for applying lime sulphur

compound to jin areas to whiten and preserve them. I use them also to colour the carved areas.
- **Electric chain saw** with 25cm (10in) blade is useful for rough shaping large-scale trunks.
- **Routers** come in many weights, descriptions and sizes, but most work in the same way. They are used for shaping and detailing jin. The cutters are a study in themselves. Pick one that is right for the job – too small is irritatingly slow; too big is clumsy. Study the different types. The key is to have something that has a smooth action.
- **Goggles** are necessary when you start using power tools.

Other Equipment

- **Water-colour paint** for tinting carved areas. I usually use tubes of designer's gouache, which is water-colour (not totally transparent) and has a little clay in the paint to give body.
- **Lime sulphur** compound is a solution painted onto newly carved jin areas. It has the quality of a preservative combined with a bleaching action and will dry pure white. I modify it to avoid that whitewashed look. It smells of rotten eggs.
- **Wound sealant** compounds are available in various Japanese pastes, which are quite good. There is a green compound called Kiyonal, which works well, providing you do not touch the bark outside the wound area. Kiyonal leaves a dark smudge. There are a couple of Japanese grey-coloured putty-like pastes, which are useful for sealing wounds. These are discreet in colour and stable, and they do not smudge. Other compounds, such as lac balsam, work well.

Containers

These are very much a case of suiting the tool to the job, and when you start, you do not need a superb bonsai container. The container limits the roots and must keep them happy and to do this it must drain perfectly and be of 'breathable' texture. This means there must be some porosity at least on the inside, so you should not use a pot that has a glazed interior.

Various plastic pots are available in the bonsai trade, and these are fine for trees in training. There are inexpensive, low-grade pots from China and Korea, which are the equivalent of the cheaper Japanese pots in quality. These can be very useful for developing a tree in a pot.

When your tree has progressed, you will need something better. I suggest suitable colours and proportions of pots and trees for each species. Although I say little about shapes except in the broadest terms, there is more about the feeling of the tree–container unit, which is what counts. Pots with a distinctive glaze or a distracting shape tend to compete with the tree, rather than add unity. Be cautious about your choice, because some pots are very seductive. Studying photographs, seeing collections and visiting shows will give you a feeling for good tree–pot combinations. In general terms the old rules of 80 per cent average thickness trunk to 20 per cent bulk of pot and 60 per cent heavy trunk to 40 per cent pot are about right. Simple ovals and rectangles are universally used. Occasionally some elaborate trunk will suggest a container that echoes something of that quality. Styles, of course, have their time-honoured combinations, like an oval for a Group, a deep pot to counterweight a Cascade and a light, small pot for a Literati tree. (The terms Group, Cascade and Literati are discussed under Bonsai Shaping, page 29.)

Viewing and Position

Bonsai need to be placed where you can see them at their best. This is on elevated shelving at least 90cm (3ft) high. You can then look directly at, rather than down on them, and this makes such a difference.

Traditional shelving arrangements call for slats that admit air and light. These look pleasant when supported on heavy plinths. I used concrete building blocks and recycled 5 × 10cm (2 × 4in) timber for the shelving, and 5 × 15cm (2 × 6in) timber for the load-carrying cross-members resting on the plinths. The timber was finished with a water-repellent, dark brown coating, formulated for use with plants. Beware of old-fashioned creosote.

If all available backgrounds are visually busy, use some quiet coloured fencing to isolate the trees. If you use a backdrop make sure the trees are well away from it.

If your site is exposed, use shade netting, which is available from most garden centres, to reduce wind velocity and sun. Plants can often tolerate certain conditions but prefer others. Shade is one such condition. You will find your plants are much happier if you shade them a little. About 30 per cent shade is fine.

In winter most flowering plants like to be frost-free or at least away from frost contact. I drape polythene curtains from the display shelving and place trees on shingle spread below the shelves. I protect apricots, cotoneasters, crab apple, firethorn, hawthorn and quinces in this way, but move azaleas, holly, pomegranates and wisteria into a plastic greenhouse (poly-tunnel). Other trees needing greenhouse protection are those that have been repotted, or extensively restyled, either by wiring or carving, or that have just been collected or any ailing trees with bad roots. Azaleas are easily affected. Protect if in doubt. In spring such trees should be shaded and kept damp. Spray the foliage.

When your plants start to bud in spring they can be put back on the shelves, but keep a watch for late frosts. You may bring your trees in for short viewing periods when they are in flower or fruit, but make it a short stay. Plants get really upset by long spells indoors when they are in active growth.

Plants displayed indoors look better if they can be enjoyed a little apart from the domestic clutter. The traditional Japanese viewing alcove provides visual isolation, and plants look very pleasing when displayed as part of the three elements of main tree, minor tree, grass or ornament, and a scroll painting. In the West, setting a plain screen behind the arrangement, with a minor plant accenting the mood of the major one and combined with a simple water-colour will achieve the same impact.

Trunk Carving

There are several ways in which carving is used to enhance the appearance of the trunk. Sometimes an area of trunk bark is deliberately peeled off to create a feeling of natural damage or shari. Some trunks may have abruptly tapered steps left over from fast trunk development. These can often be corrected by using a chain saw or router either to smooth the transitional area or to create the feeling of natural driftwood by carving the area to enhance the form and open the grain of the wood. Other trees may be carved to create additional bends or splits in the trunk. Provided it is not overdone, the technique is useful in adding to the atmosphere of the image.

A field-grown tree with rotted stumps from branch and trunk pruning.

A router is used to carve out the stumps and make a more flowing trunk profile.

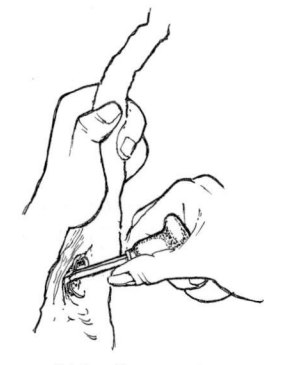

Engraving tools are useful for finer carving.

In nature, flowering and fruiting species often develop hollows in the trunk, perhaps where branches are damaged or ripped off. Such hollowed areas, or uro, can be used to advantage where a branch is scheduled for removal. Then, instead of a man-made sealed cut, you gain the interest of a shadowed cavity, which is carefully shaped to blend with the trunk. Routers are useful for making hollows.

The trick with most wood sculpture is to begin coarse and finish fine. Bonsai are no exception. Because the carved wood is, for the most part, green, it is important to phase the operation so that both the rough carving and the finer operations are followed by a natural drying interval. Green wood carves with all the crispness of a face-cloth! Allowed to dry, it carves as sweetly as sharpening a pencil – it is worth the wait.

When you have finished carving, it is time to consider treating the area with lime sulphur solution to preserve and bleach it. When it is wet, lime sulphur is a violent yellow, but once it has dried it has a decided whitening effect.

I usually apply some grey-black water-colour to the wood at this point. Use a light covering and concentrate on toning down the bright colour of the wood. Apply darker paint in the recesses and lighter paint on the raised areas. If you use your nails or a rake, you can open lines in the colour that exactly replicate the grain. Let the paint dry thoroughly before you apply lime sulphur, and if, after the lime sulphur has dried, the painting is obscured, just do it again on top – it will stay there a while and weather in nicely.

Note: be careful not to peel the bark too close to the root line because this can cause the roots to die back.

Branch Carving
This technique is widely applied to conifers but not as much to flowering and deciduous trees, presumably because the wood of flowering trees is softer and would rot away, rather than remain as lasting forms. Called jin, such peeled and carved redundant

branches can, in the right context, have great decorative value.

If the tree seems to need some branch thinning, it can be interesting to convert a couple to jin. The method is to limit the peeled area by circling the bark with a scalpel, cutting down to the wood. The bark is then squashed by nipping it with jin pliers. This frees the bark and it can be peeled easily. The peeled branch is carved to suit the design. If the wood is heavy it may need to dry out between

The effect of sympathetic carving has been to add 'ageing' detail.

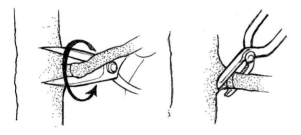

Left: to convert a live branch to jin, first ring the bark.
Right: free the bark by squashing it with jin pliers.

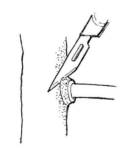

Trim up the base with a scalpel.

Peeling live bark to make a Shari. Adding a jin.

carving sessions. Jin may be wired into position. Once the wood has dried out, the shape will hold. The jin is then coloured and treated like the *shari*.

Note: in any carving of bonsai, remember you are reproducing the effect of weather-beaten age. Do not finish the wood so smoothly that it resembles French-polished furniture, and do not make it so uniformly white that it looks artificial. Age and the illusion of age are all about texture and a worn appearance. That is why I have laid such emphasis on the importance of the whole image, not just on one technique.

Propagation

Air Layering Air layering is an easy technique that enables you to pick a well-shaped branch or trunk section on the donor plant. Begin with something 'aged' and exciting, with the bonus that the wood is mature and of flower-bearing age.

You will need: scalpel, jin pliers, rooting hormone (powder or solution), sphagnum moss, string, clear plastic sheet, black plastic sheet and plastic string or fine wire.
Season: early spring.

Assess your material and pick a section with some gnarled character. The would-be rooting zone works best if it is located beneath side branches.

Make two cuts, about 2.5cm (1in) apart, with the scalpel, ringing the base of your chosen section and making sure you cut through the bark. The bark between the rings is then squashed and removed by gripping it with jin pliers.

If your chosen section is less than 2.5cm (1in) thick, you may want to cut an incomplete ring, pre-serving a bridge of live bark. This prevents the section from drying up. If the section is thick, make the ringing cuts further apart – the distance between them should be three times the diameter of the section.

Treat the peeled area with rooting hormone and wrap it thickly with damp sphagnum moss. Make sure the main mossed area is below the peeled zone to induce the new roots to grow out and down, not up. You may find it convenient to keep the moss in place with some loosely tied string. Wrap the moss in clear plastic. Wrap again with black plastic, which accentuates the greenhouse effect by efficiently absorbing warmth from the sun. Secure with plastic string or light wire. Tie the string securely around the branch, both above and below the layer to keep in moisture. The layer must not dry out.

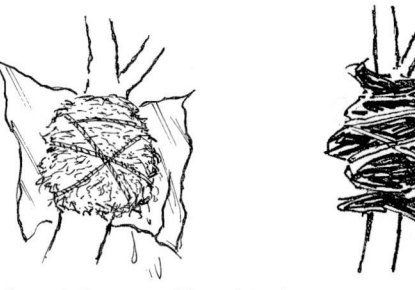

Left: pack the area with moist sphagnum moss and cover it with clear plastic film. **Right:** add an outer cover of black plastic sheet for heat absorption.

Check after a month or so for the initial signs of roots, white tips poking through the moss. To do this, you will have to remove the outer black plastic layer. Check that the moss is still moist. If you find signs of roots, you will have to leave them to grow and multiply for a while longer. Take off the outer black plastic and if there seems to be a lot of mois-ture locked inside the inner, clear film, you can aerate the moss by poking holes in the plastic.

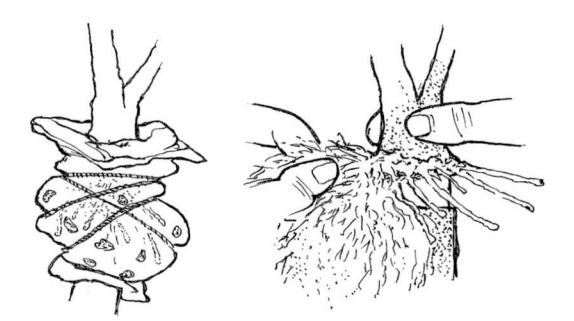

Left: remove the black plastic as roots appear and make holes in the clear plastic for air and drainage. **Right:** before detaching the layer, carefully remove the moss.

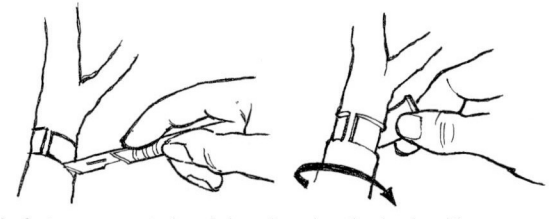

Left: to propagate by air layering, ring the bark with a scalpel, keeping a bark bridge. **Right:** peel away the bark.

Dust the area with hormone rooting powder.

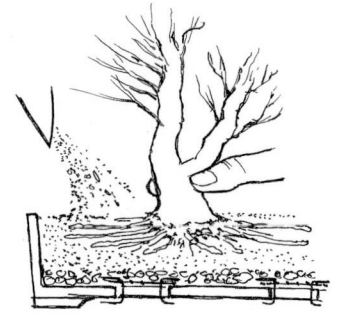

Pot up in open soil, taking care to spread the roots and support the trunk.

Most of the species in the book will root well inside the season. Some, such as Chinese and Japanese quinces, root very quickly, making it possible to detach them inside a couple of months.

Once the clear plastic appears to be fairly well filled with roots, you can detach the layer and plant it up. Make sure you do this in shady conditions and keep the layer there subsequently. A plastic greenhouse is ideal. Use a container that is large enough to accept the roots when they have been spread out and prepare it as you would a bonsai pot, with good drainage and a light soil.

Very gently tease out the roots, which will be tangled in the moss. At this stage, the new roots are the same texture as bean sprouts, but more brittle, so take your time. removing as much of the moss as you can without breaking the roots. Spread the roots as well as you can on the bed of soil, then pot up in the usual way. Water in well and then ease back on soil watering. Foliage spray is useful.

After a month or so of growth, if the leaves look good and you see new shoots, you can assume your work is successful. Do not feed in the first year. In year 2 feed with half-strength 0–10–10 throughout the season. Even if you see flower buds forming, it is a good idea to remove them, to give the layer a chance to make a good start. After a couple of seasons of good growth, repot the tree into an appropriate pot and let it flower.

Cuttings Cuttings are an excellent way of increasing your stock of a favourite plant or some special variety. Material of different thicknesses may be rooted, so you can create all sorts of interest in, for example, a Group, right at the very first stage.

You can insert 'bunch' cuttings, which, as the name suggests, are multi-stemmed pieces obtained by slicing material beneath a whorl of shoots and inserting the whole thing. You can, of course, initiate any of the styles (see page 29) at the cutting stage if you wish, simply by pre-working your cutting into shape.

Another exciting aspect of cuttings is that they offer an opportunity to make some first-class miniature bonsai. If you take thick cuttings from a wall shrub of Japanese quince, for instance, you can often trim these before insertion and get short, gnarled 'trunks' complete with branches! As with air layering, the wood comes 'aged' and capable of flowering almost immediately.

> **You will need:** shears, paper towels, plastic bags, plastic seed trays (preferably with clear plastic lids), peat and sand insertion mixture, scalpel or scissors, rooting hormone (powder or solution) and fungicide.
> **Season:** early spring to summer.

Assess your material and plan it. Gather it using the shears, wrap it in damp paper towels and place it inside a plastic bag. Put the bag in a refrigerator while you prepare the seed trays.

Fill the seed trays to the brim with an insertion mix of 50 per cent peat and 50 per cent sand. Tamp the mixture flat. Submerge the tray in water until air bubbles stop rising and then drain it well.

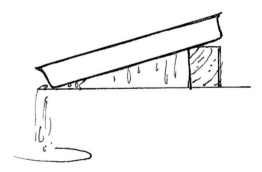

Fill the tray with the peat and sand mixture, water well and drain away the surplus.

Take your material from the refrigerator and prepare it. This is the creative bit because you assess each piece for bonsai possibilities. In general terms, each cutting must be inserted deeply enough to stand when it is firmed in. That means that if your cutting is destined for life as a miniature bonsai, with an overall height of 8cm (3in), you need a cutting of 10cm (4in) to allow for good anchorage of 2.5cm (1in) in the tray. The cutting will root around the soil line and anything below that is unwanted is removed.

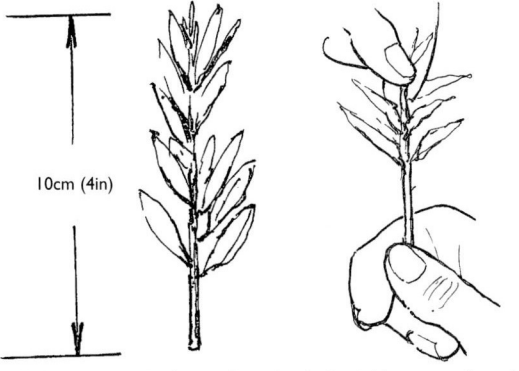

Left: to propagate by cuttings begin by taking a cutting about
10cm (4in) long. **Right:** pinch out the soft growing tip.

Remove the leaves from the lower part of the
cutting so that air can circulate around it when it is
inserted. When all the material is prepared, re-cut
the bases using a scalpel or sharp scissors. Dip each
one into the rooting hormone and insert it into the
medium. You may find it helpful to make holes
prior to insertion. Do not push the cuttings in too
deeply because it is important that they do not
touch the bottom of the tray. Firm them in and
water them in well. Spray with fungicide.

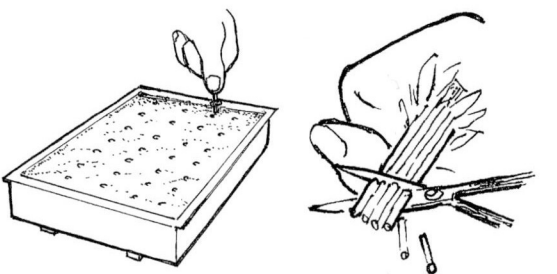

Left: use a nail to make regularly spaced insertion holes over
the compost. **Right:** re-cut the bases of the cuttings and apply
rooting hormone.

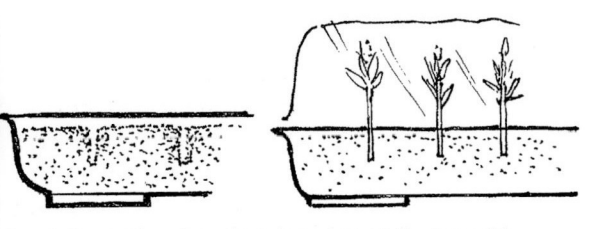

Insert the cuttings, firm them in and cover the tray with
pierced plastic.

Place the plastic lids over the cuttings and put
the trays under a bench in the greenhouse where
they get light shade. Most plastic lids are fitted with
rotating air-vents – make sure these are open.

After a few days, check for moisture and look
for any fallen leaves and remove them. Repeat the
fungicidal spray every two weeks or so. Leave the
lids ajar periodically for extra ventilation, but do not
let the cuttings get too dry.

I have known quince cuttings to root in about
three weeks. Look first for callusing, a swelling of
the treated area, which is followed by root initials,
white pointed tips just poking out from the wall of
the cutting, which you can find by having a gentle
'test pull'! Callusing material resists.

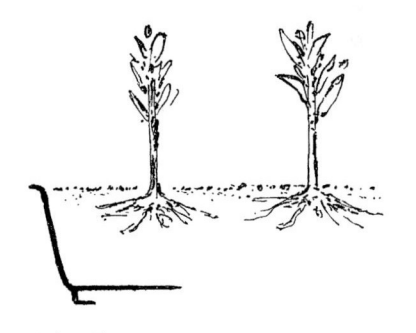

The rooted cuttings.

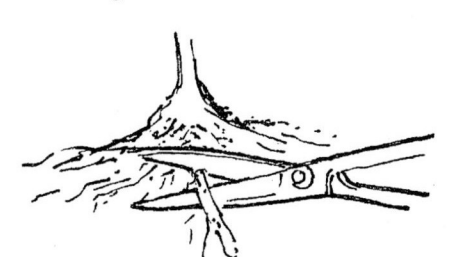

Even the roots.

Transplant the cuttings, spreading the roots in the pot.

After rooting is noticed, allow another couple of weeks and then cautiously lift a cutting and see what sort of roots you have. If they are good, you can transplant the cuttings into a container with plenty of root development space, which should be filled with light soil, and pot them up. Use containers that are broad and wide rather than deep.

If the cuttings are still not strongly rooted or are just swelling, give them more time. Every species behaves slightly differently. The degree of 'take' with cuttings has a lot to do with the age of the donor tree, which should ideally be no more than five years old, because young material is full of vigour.

Take great care to spread the roots when you transplant the cuttings. Trim any taproots in the making, water in well and replace the individual containers under the bench. Ease back on soil watering but spray the foliage.

After a month or so of growth, if the leaves and new shoots look strong, give them half-strength 0–10–10 once a month until midsummer.

In year 2 the slow rooters may well be strongly rooted and can be transplanted. Run all the cuttings for a season 'on their own roots' before working with them as bonsai. It gives them the best start, and they will soon overtake plants that were prematurely worked.

Timing and Method The optimum timing and method of taking cuttings for each species discussed in Part II are described below.

APRICOT Take well-grown 13cm (5in) cuttings in autumn and store them in a frost-free green house, buried in moist sand. Seal the top and pre-cut the base of each cutting so that a primary callus can form over winter. In early spring, check the cuttings for signs of calluses. Dip those that have developed calluses in rooting hormone and insert them in moistened peat and sand mix in containers that are deep enough to allow clearance below the cuttings. Firm them in and water well. Growth should be strong after a month or so. Discard any cuttings that are not callused and those that do not grow strongly.

AZALEA Take new shoots when they have made at least 8cm (3in) of growth. This is usually in late spring or early summer. Remove leaves from the lower part of the cuttings. Trim the bases, treat with rooting hormone and insert in moistened peat and sand mix to half their depth, and firm in. Water well with a fine spray and place them under a bench in the greenhouse. Treat with fungicide. They may need a plastic bag over the tray to maintain humidity.

COTONEASTER Take strongly grown 8–10cm (3–4in) shoot cuttings in late spring. Trim the bases and remove the lower leaves. Treat with rooting hormone and insert in moistened peat and sand. Aftercare is standard.

CRAB APPLE Take strongly grown 15–20cm (6–8in) cuttings of previous year's wood in early spring. Seal the top and cut the base of each cutting. Treat with rooting hormone and insert in moistened peat and sand in containers deep enough to accept half the cutting with bottom clearance. Aftercare is standard.

FIRETHORN As for cotoneaster.

HAWTHORN Some species root better than others. Try treating as for crab apple.

DECIDUOUS HOLLY As for cotoneaster and crab apple – that is, current and previous year's wood.

POMEGRANATE As for azalea.

QUINCE As for cotoneaster, but you can also take heavy grade wood.

WISTERIA As for crab apple. Select cuttings with some bends in them.

Seedlings This is the slowest method of propagation and, because cuttings of most of the included species are obtainable and are faster, I have included the method for sowing seed of the American deciduous holly (*Ilex verticillata*) as a typical case.

Pick ripe berries in late autumn and spread them out to dry. They are placed in warm moist sand and stratified to obtain the best germination. Seeds are stratified by placing them in a seed tray filled with clean, moistened sand. They should be lightly covered with sand and then stored at 21°C (70°F). for two months and then at 4°C (40°F) for two months.

Plant in seed trays in spring when stratification is finished. Fill seed trays with a moistened half peat and half sand, and plant the holly seed in rows on the surface. Cover with 3mm (⅛ in) light soil, and water in using a very fine spray.

Place the trays under a bench in a greenhouse. Germination should start in another two months. As the seedlings appear, give them more light and spray them with fungicide to combat damping off. Hollies are usually strong and will grow well. Grow them undisturbed in the trays for a year and then transplant them for another year of development. Bonsai training can begin in the third year.

Grafts Grafting is another reliable way of increasing your stock of chosen bonsai material. It has the advantages of giving a weaker scion some push from the understock (rootstock) and an immediate trunk buttress and root spread to a young plant.

The understocks should be on the move and the scions still dormant for the very best results. The easiest grafting method for our purposes is the simple side graft.

The understock and scion can be used to create a smooth grafted line if you choose material of identical thicknesses. If in-built taper is desired, a heavier understock will begin this for you.

Root-prune the understock and cut it back to 5–8cm (2–3in) from the roots. Match the scions to the understock and make sure there are at least four leaf buds on each scion. Make a long and a short cut on the base of each scion, creating a lop-sided V. The V-shaped wedge should be about 18mm (¾in) on the long cut and 6mm (¼in) on the shorter cut.

You will need: two-year-old understocks, freshly gathered scions (about 8cm (3in) long), shears, scalpel, expanding plastic tape, wound sealant.
Season: early spring is best.

Kurume azalea.

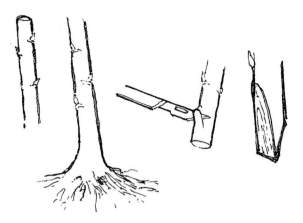

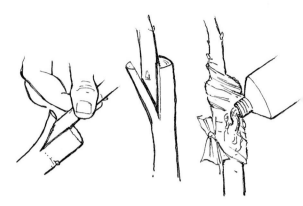

Left: choose the scion and understock for grafting.
Centre: trim the scion. **Right:** the scion is trimmed with
short and long cuts.

Left: insert the scion with the long cut inwards. **Centre:** the
edge of the cambium layer must be carefully aligned.
Right: the graft is secured with tape and sealed.

Make a cut, 18mm (³⁄₄ in) deep, in the understock with a scalpel. Viewed from overhead, the cut
should be made across the one o'clock and five
o'clock points of the understock section.

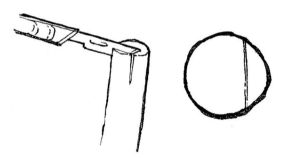

The understock is trimmed square and then split from one
o'clock to five o'clock.

Open the understock and insert the scion,
matching the long cuts together. The long cut faces
into the scion. Make sure that you line up at least
one set of cambium layers on scion and understock.
The thinner graft type should line up on both sides.
Take time to ensure a good fit.

Wrap the graft with the expanding plastic tape,
taking care not to shift the graft, and smear Kiyonal
wound sealant over the area to make it airtight. Pot
the grafts in individual containers with well-drained
soil. Water in well and shade the grafts, placing them

in a warm plastic greenhouse. After about a month
to six weeks, you should start to see growth push
and you can gradually wean the grafts away from
the shade and increase the air flow. Grow the grafts
vigorously in the first year and feed well, but keep
them in the plastic greenhouse (poly-tunnel).

In the spring of year 2 the grafts can be transplanted into shallower, wider containers and the
trunks can be shortened to give a change of growth
direction and enhance taper. The plastic wrapping
tape is removed at this point. Grow the grafts in the

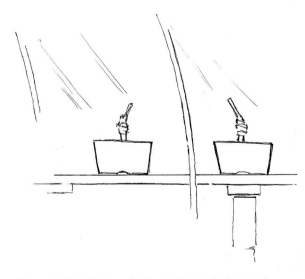

Keep potted grafts in a plastic greenhouse (poly-tunnel).

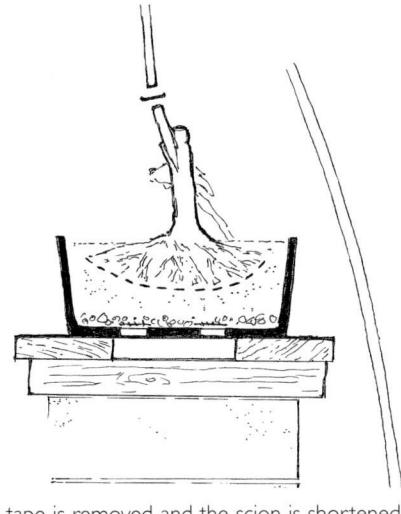

Year 2: the tape is removed and the scion is shortened.

The graft is developing into a tree.

plastic greenhouse for another season to make sure there are no sudden drops in the humidity around the graft.

In the spring of year 3 the grafts are transplanted again and the shoots are cut back adjacent to outward-facing buds. This automatically changes the growth direction. Grow the trees as they are now vigorously for another season, then, in year 4, the plants are ready for wire shaping. First, trim the growth back to outward-facing buds and, as the growth extends, wire it very gently to add some curves to the basically angular forms.

That is the basic method that broadly applies to apricot, crab apple and hawthorn. Grafted wisteria

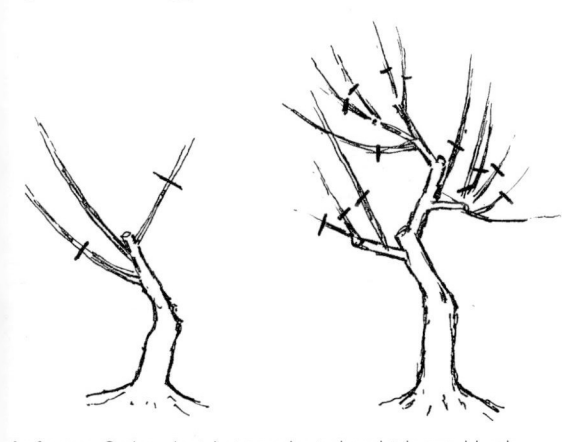

Left: year 3: the plant is transplanted and trimmed back.
Right: year 4: trim back growth and wire new shoots.

are best grown as suggested in Seasonal Care (see pages 119–21).

UNDERSTOCKS

Apricot: *Prunus cerasifera* Myrobalan Group (cherry plum)

Crab apple: *Malus pumila* (wild apple)

Red hawthorn: *Crataegus laevigata* (syn. *C. oxyacantha*) 'Paul's Scarlet' (hawthorn)

Wisteria cultivar: onto Japanese or Chinese type understocks as appropriate

Division As the name suggests, this is a way of utilizing a lot of overgrown material. The technique has been followed by gardeners for generations as a way of multiplying plants that are multi-stemmed or that have roots that produce a lot of suckers.

From the bonsai grower's point of view, division is a way of capitalizing on a lot of material that would otherwise be wasted at root-pruning time. Heavy roots can be pruned and re-grown as plants, and in breaking up a clump of overgrown material lies the chance of finding a natural raft or root-connected plant.

You will need: shears, fine scissors, branch cutters, turntable, rake, soil sieve, potting soil, saw, wound sealant, prepared containers and tying-in wires.
Season: early spring.

There are four main methods.

1. Multi-trunked plants that are well supplied with roots can be divided by cutting the trunks apart at the base, creating separately rooted trunks.

Division: method 1.

2. Plants that produce basal suckers from the surface roots can have a percentage of the roots removed complete with shoots and feeder roots below. Sectioned up or left entire, they can produce raft and root-connected trees.

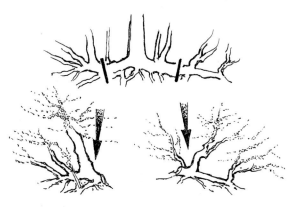

Division: method 2.

3. Some plants bud from the roots below the soil, close to the trunk, and these can be split away and planted as trees.

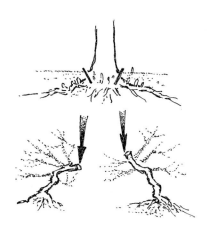

Division: method 3.

4. Root runners that have feeder roots hanging from them can be sectioned up and started as separate plants.

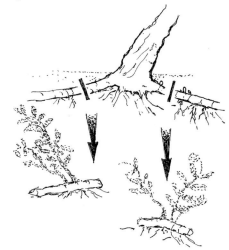

Division: method 4.

Among the species that can be developed by division are the crab apple, hawthorn, pomegranate, quince and wisteria; they can be propagated by the method indicated: crab apple – 2 and 3; hawthorn – 2; pomegranate – 2; quince – 1, 2 and 3; wisteria – 4.

The desired section is separated and individually potted according to the style it suggests. The triple-trunk quince 'Toyonishiki', for example, which is shown on page 116, began life as a method 2 tree.

Division can also give you fascinating miniature bonsai. A gnarled root section can yield a crab apple, hawthorn, pomegranate or quince bonsai no taller than 8–10cm (3–4in)! How many wisterias can you get from those heavy root runners?

As with all newly potted bonsai, treat divisions to a little after care and you will have some beautiful, characterful plants in a year or two.

Bonsai Shaping

The easiest way to appreciate bonsai is to see them. Visit exhibitions and societies and bonsai nurseries, particularly those that import plants. Study pictures of good trees. There are many photographic annuals available through the bonsai trade that show good quality Japanese bonsai. Pictures are second best because they are two-dimensional, so study them in winter when you cannot get out to see the real thing.

'Seeing' involves walking around a bonsai and checking its three-dimensional aspect. Let the features sink in one by one. Be aware of trunk quality and line, branch position, shape and taper, roots and their formation and structural support of the trunk, neat foliage texture, pot shape and colour and, lastly, the flowers or fruit.

When you start, things will register with you in anything but that order! You will see the flowers. With flowering trees that is a major point of appreciation, of course, but it is not the only criterion by which a tree is judged. So what are the others? The answer is that many elements contribute to a well-trained tree. Depth of content is what it is all about. How the grower – or perhaps more than one grower – has added a wealth of detail but kept them contained by the whole – like every good art at work.

Details in the tree and the way in which they have been used are fascinating. Suppose we look at these elements more closely to try and understand them and how the owner or owners can make them work. We need to look first at the shapes used in bonsai.

Bonsai Shapes

The fact that most of the classic bonsai follow no predetermined shape probably explains their magical charm. Certainly the old rigid styles have largely been replaced with guidelines for a tree that is naturally arranged, in a form suited to the species.

Informal Upright: a Japanese flowering apricot planted in the Root on Rock style.

It is as such that I have included the following shape descriptions, which I consider work with the species described in Part II.

Most bonsai are trained to be around 46–60cm (18–24in) in height when finished. This is a convenient size for moving around and viewing. Some trees are much larger than this – their size usually being determined by their height when collected.

Informal Upright Informal Upright, as the name suggests, is based on the gently curved trunks and forms of meadow and woodland trees. It has a pleasantly three-dimensional, curved trunk. The curves are slow and graceful, with the longest of them in the lower trunk. The curves get closer together and shorter as the trunk ascends. The upper part quite often slopes forwards, so that the trunk is inclined gently forwards, creating extra depth through the design. Branches are encouraged to sweep outwards and downwards from the bends in the trunk, mostly in an alternating arrangement. Some are trained to the back for depth in the design. Branches are curved to echo those in the trunk. The leaf profiles are mostly gently domed. There is a pervasive naturalness in this design. The outline of the tree is roughly triangular. This happens to look natural and it gives a pleasing result. This outline and style also

Leaning: crab apple.

Cascade: wisteria.

work with most of the species discussed in Part II.

You will soon note that this style varies tremendously in appearance when it is applied to trees with different kinds of trunks, such as extra thick or thin, tall or short, craggy or smooth. These features are often used as a highlight in the design, as a visual focus. Older, well-trained bonsai often have natural highlights such as trunk hollows, rough or smooth and shining bark, some extraordinary branch of unusual shape or length and so on.

The deciduous, flowering trees may also be styled so that, when out of leaf, they have a validity of form. Such examples will be twiggier and more densely branched. Cotoneaster can look very pleasing like this. Use oval or rectangular pots.

Leaning In this form the trunk is raked over at an angle of about 30 degrees or so. The shape is based on the image of trees growing on a steep hillside. It is very like the Informal Upright but with modified branch lines that sweep outwards in the same way, then take on a more horizontal angle to balance the thrust of the trunk. Quite often there will be a longer branch that compensates for the angle of the trunk by taking the eye back over the centre line. Use oval pots.

There are great advantages to be gained from styling such a tree with wooden wedges propping

the pot. A friend of mine uses floppy bean bags, which work extremely well. When it is in position, you can check the new angle of the trunk and also where you will have to modify the branch length/angle to balance the form.

Trees worth considering for this shape are apricot, azalea, cotoneaster, crab apple, firethorn, hawthorn, pomegranate and wisteria.

Semi-cascade and Cascade These trees follow the shapes of mountain survivors. The trunk line of the Cascade tree falls over and below the base of the pot, often curving back on itself. The trunk form can be rippled or straightish. The branches occur on

Semi-cascade: hawthorn.

Literati: Japanese flowering apricot.

Driftwood: azalea.

outer bends and are arranged so that they step down and rotate around the axis of the trunk.

The Semi-cascade tree follows the same basic idea, but the trunk does not go below the pot. Use deepish square or round pots. Most of the species (except the holly) look well in either style.

Literati The name for this style came from the trees depicted in paintings by men of letters, the Literati. It is a style like the visual short-hand of the original drawings. Trunks are simple and full of energy, like the brush stroke. Branches are few and the foliage is thinned, so that just a suggestion is made. Trunk shapes are free, and the small pot is simple and understated.

Many of the species included can be thinned out and grown in this style. Deciduous holly is outstanding.

Driftwood There is almost a style developing these days based on a trunk patterned by carving. The original inspiration for these are trees that have survived mountain hazards and carry the scars from hurricanes, earthquakes and avalanches. Trunks are often split, gouged out and hollowed but spiralled with a thread-like vein of live bark to keep the sap flowing.

The exposed wood dries out and bleaches, and gives a tremendously strong impression of age, particularly when contrasted with fresh new foliage. When

they are collected, driftwood trees are first carefully re-established. Training usually consists of developing enough foliage to style into shapes that pick up and echo the curves and character of the trunk.

Apricot, crab apple, firethorn and pomegranate make good driftwood trees. Pots should tie the elements of the design together and can be quite forceful as a result. Ovals and rectangles are commonly used.

Rock Grown There are two types of rock planting: the first is where the tree sits in a saddle of the stone with the roots trained over it, their tips buried in soil in the container below. The second is when

Root over Rock: cotoneaster.

Root on rock: azalea standing in a suiban on a bed of sand

Root Connected: flowering quince.

Raft: pomegranate.

the plant is confined entirely to the rock, the container used is called a *suiban* and is sometimes filled with water or fine gravel. Most of the species mentioned look beautiful in either variation. Pots for Root over Rock are usually shallow – ovals or rectangles both work – and the same shapes are used for *suiban* with trees grown on a rock.

Raft The trunk in this style is laid down on the soil and the branches take over as tree trunks. The name comes from the raised spine of the old trunk, which someone thought resembled a raft. Roots are induced to pop out from the recumbent trunk, and as soon as they have sufficiently grown, the old root system is removed or is greatly reduced. The branches/trees are trained into a group arrangement and the artificial arrangement soon looks natural.

Cotoneaster, crab apple, holly, hawthorn and quince all look lovely as a Raft group.

Root-connected This is a style formed quite naturally by those trees that sucker freely, such as azalea, crab apple and quince. When such a tree is damaged,

a multitude of root suckers and basal shoots are produced. This shape forms the inspiration for the style. In bonsai the suckers and shoots are thinned out and styled to appear as grouped trunks.

Group The inspiration for this style is woodland. Trunks are arranged to create spatial perspective in such a manner that no two actually cross each other and block the view. Trunk shapes that harmonize with each other are chosen and used as thick and thin linear accents, with wide and narrower negative areas between them. Odd numbers of trunks are

Group: deciduous holly.

Twin-trunk: firethorn.

Shohin: cotoneaster

traditionally planted. Cotoneaster and hawthorn make wonderful Group bonsai.

Containers for Raft, Root-connected and Group styles are pretty similar: they are shallow in the main and the oval is the best shape because it harmonizes easily. Use generously sized containers because it is important to create implied open space.

Twin-trunk This shape is a tribute to gentle meadow trees, and it suits the natural habit of flowering trees admirably. There is usually a main and minor trunk line. The shape can be fairly free, and, like the Informal Upright in feeling, the pattern of branch lines makes a dialogue between the trunks. It is a style that can work with many different sizes and textures of trunks, as long as you keep the two separate in thickness.

This shape works with all the species.

Small Bonsai: *Mame* **or** *Shohin* As the name suggests, these can be tiny – no more than a few inches even when potted – and it is an area where flowering and fruiting trees can shine. You will be working with small-featured cultivars, such as the dwarf flowering quince (*Chaenomeles japonica* 'Chojubai'). The dwarf pomegranate (*Punica granatum* var. *nana*) makes an attractive small tree and so does *Cotoneaster horizontalis*. There are tiny fruited crab apples and dwarf deciduous hollies, one with pinhead- and one with matchhead-size red berries.

Sources of Material

There are four sources of material for flowering bonsai: naturally dwarfed wild trees; container-grown nursery stock; imported bonsai; and quick-grown bonsai that are raised by propagation.

Wild Trees

You will need: spade, shears, trowel, branch pruners, rake, hessian (burlap), 8cm (3in) nails, polythene sheet, containers with good drainage holes, crocking screen, potting soil (the proportions for each species is included in Seasonal Care; 50 per cent sand and 50 per cent organic material will work for this purpose).
Season: early spring.

The standard method is to dig a double trench around the tree preserving an inner circle with a diameter of at least 30cm (12in). Under-cut the area. Lift the soil out between the spade-cut circles

When collecting wild trees, dig a double trench.

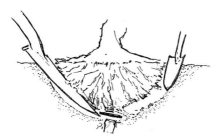

Clear the soil and sever the taproot.

Reduce the branch load.

Wrap the roots for transportation.

and check the exposed roots. If the inner soil area hangs together well and a mixture of root sizes is exposed it should be safe to lift the tree. Clear the soil out under the rootball and sever the taproot. Wrap the rootball with moist hessian (burlap) and secure it with nails pushed through the root mass. Add a layer of polythene if you have any distance to travel.

If the exposed roots in the double trench look coarse and the tree is loose inside the spade circle, add some potting soil to the open trench and leave the tree until next spring. It will by then have made finer roots. Reduce the branch load to keep a

balance with the smaller root mass. If you cannot easily get back, there is a technique invented by Dan Robinson of Washington, 'Robinson's Root Enhancement', that will really help.

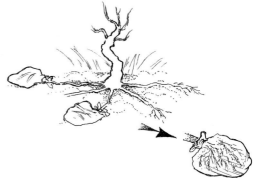

Dan Robinson's root enhancement method.

Dan's method is to find and follow all the root lines outward from the trunk until fine roots are located. These are carefully dug out, wrapped in polythene bags that have been filled with bonsai soil, watered and left on the surface in the sun. The warmth creates mini-greenhouses inside the plastic bags, which fill with root!

When you get back home, clean ragged root ends.

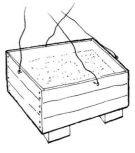

Prepare a growing box that is large enough to take the root mass.

When you get back home, treat any ragged branch cuts or damaged root ends by cutting them so that they are clean. Seal large cuts with tree wound paint. Put the tree in dappled shade or rig up a tent of shade netting. You can either plant the tree in the ground, prepared by forking in some potting soil, or plant it in a growing box large enough to accept the root mass without disturbance.

The tree will suffer from transplant shock and will need some extra care. Tie it into the container or stake it in the ground. If the tree is static, the roots take hold better. Give the tree some vitamin B1 transplant solution in the initial and second soil watering. Mist the top of the tree with a periodic water spray. Think of the tree as an enormous cutting: it needs a moist head and damp, but not

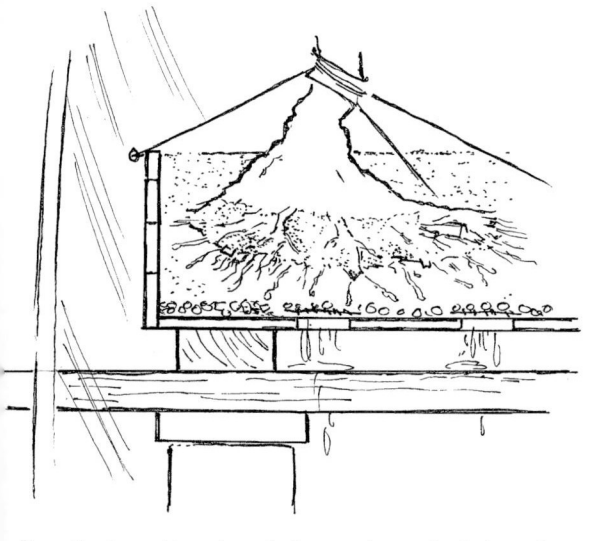

Place the boxed tree in a plastic greenhouse (poly-tunnel)

soggy roots. Conserve the moisture around the tree with a polythene tent if necessary or grow it in a poly-tunnel greenhouse.

Do not feed in the first year. In the following spring, if you see signs of leaf growth, you can feed the tree with half-strength 0–10–10. Give weak feeds every three weeks or so until the tree is obviously happy. If you feel decided resistance (indicating good root growth) when you try to gently rock the trunk, this is the time to consider some basic styling – but not before!

Container-grown Nursery Stock

You will need: shears, branch pruners, fine scissors, rake, aluminium training wire, wire cutters, potting soil, soil sieve, wound sealant compound, containers.
Season: anytime. Always style first and pot later; potting is best done in spring.

Choose plants with stocky lower trunks with some curving movement and strong lower branching. Trunk taper is a bonus, but this can be induced by shortening the trunk and re-growing the line using a branch. Existing branches can be sacrificed and more suitable ones grown in their place.

Check that the leaf colour is good and that there are no browned areas. Check for signs of insect damage.

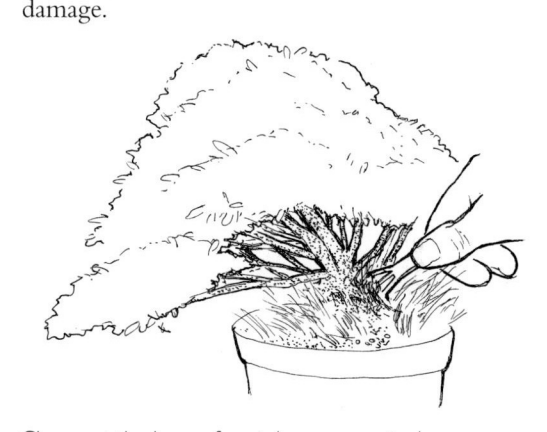

Clean out the base of container-grown stock.

You should begin by clearing the soil surface of fallen leaves and weeds. Work down with a rake and expose any surface roots. Now you get the first real look at the tree and the quality of the image you can make. Examine how the trunk is shaped. Is it squat and heavy, thin and curvy, multi-trunked, multi-branched, and is it straight or bent? Does it have interesting bark or a conspicuous trunk character? There is a lot to look for, so you should take your time.

If you find any insect damage, you should check for any remaining bugs. The most common are the scale insect, the mealy bug and the woolly aphid.

The base is a mass of shoots.

At this point you might find that adapting what you see to one of the bonsai styles suggests a solution or two. Later, as you gain confidence, you will work more freely with the tree, taking the trunk as the sculptural core and hanging the branch structure onto it to express some aspect of the tree that excites you.

Prune redundant branches.

Wire the remaining branches.

Prune and arrange the trunk and branches according to your plan, then wire coil the areas to be altered and bend them into position. When your arrangement is finished, you can then move on to considering a pot. Do *not* pot the tree at this point. Your tree will develop at twice the rate if you let it be a tree and just grow for a while. Give it a season of feeding and good watering. It has probably been short of both in a commercial nursery.

Next spring prepare your chosen pot. Secure crocking screens over the drainage holes by looping wire ties through them. Pass tie wires up through the drainage holes and drape them over the pot rim. These are twisted over the base of the trunk when the tree is planted to help hold and locate the tree at the new angle. Add a drainage course of 6mm ($\frac{1}{4}$ in) grade sand.

Ease the tree out of the pot. You may have to tap the plastic nursery pot a few times to loosen the root mass. If the tree has been in the pot for a while, you will find a circle of heavy roots at the bottom of the pot.

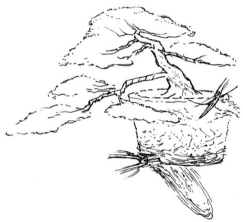

Sort out the roots. Note the root collar!

Start by removing this collar of root. Prune it away and start teasing out the smaller coiled roots. The object is to even the root mass, so prune older, lower roots to encourage the growth of fine feeder roots. Compare the future pot with the root mass and use this as a guide as you prune. Do not take too much. If the roots almost touch the pot wall when the tree is in the pot, that is enough.

Add a layer of soil mix and try the tree in position. Spread the roots so that they radiate from the trunk. If you are using a pot with a significant major axis, it is usual to plant the tree off-centre, sometimes at about the one-third mark. The trunk is also placed slightly behind the centre line. Both these arrangements are pleasing to the eye. If the tree shape is biased to the left it is planted to the right so that it dominates the left-hand two-thirds of the pot space or vice versa. Semi-cascade, Cascade and Literati bonsai are usually centrally placed to balance the weight of the first two styles and the energy of the last.

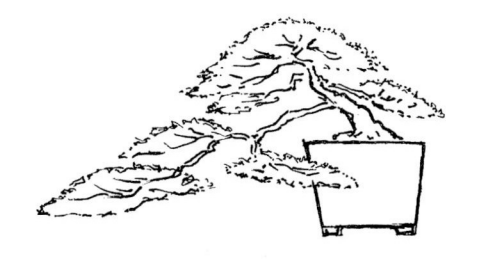

The final view, which it is quite possible to achieve in a session.

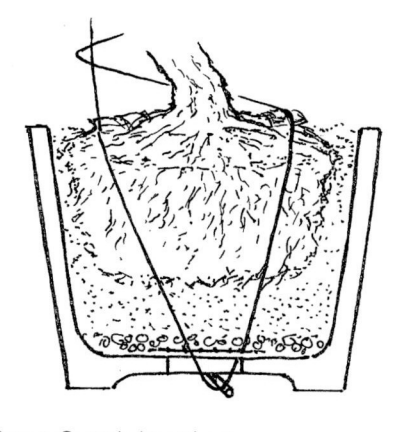

Pot up into a Cascade bonsai pot.

Check the height of the root mass as you plant the tree. Do not lose the surface roots, but prune the bottom of the root mass flat so that it sits well in the pot. Check the angle of the trunk and, if it needs tilting, add more soil under the flattened root surface until you have the right posture. Once you are happy with the angle and height of the tree in the pot, bring the tie wires over the main surface roots, from left to right and right to left to secure the tree and twist tie them. Continue adding soil until the pot is almost filled, leaving a gap of about 3mm (⅛in) below the rim for watering. Use the rake to smooth the edges of the root mass to avoid a line of old root. As you pot take care to avoid air pockets in the root mass. If you even the roots properly, however, this should not be a problem and the tree will sit well.

Place the tree on a shelf in dappled shade and brush away any residue of roots and soil. When the soil surface is smooth, water in the tree. Use a fine spray of water and let it play gently so that it does not erode the soil before it settles. When you see

muddy water puddling under the pot, the soil is saturated. Delay further watering until the soil shows signs of drying.

Imported Bonsai There are several reasons for buying a ready-made tree. It might be of some really desirable variety, which can be used in a dual capacity as a stock plant. It might also be a half-developed plant that you can have fun in training. It might be a specimen tree that you must have, although try to choose trees that leave room for your own ideas. Some of the trees shown later in the book are imported trees that have been improved. It is an interesting aspect of bonsai that has not been discussed.

Maturing bonsai from Japan are offered as semi-specimens, in more than one grade, and as specimen trees. The semi-specimen tree usually has a well-shaped trunk and good branching, but the development of the branch system has not gone far. The tree is often all trunk and sometimes this is extremely thick. Size is no criterion in bonsai. A big trunk without taper is just big. Quality is to do with proportion, not size.

The trunk may have stepped taper, which occurs when a field-grown tree is chopped back and re-grown, creating steps in the trunk line. Try to find one where the taper is not too abrupt. A bonus with semi-specimen trees that are planted in akadama soil is that the trunk base may be covered, and there is often a buried treasure of thickened surface roots ready to be utilized in the design.

Specimen trees are variable in quality, but excellent trees are still exported. In the species that interest us there are a lot to choose from. Look for apricot, Satsuki azalea, cotoneaster, crab apple, firethorn, Japanese hawthorn and deciduous holly. Most of

Flowers of the white Japanese flowering apricot.

these are available, together with less familiar trees like mulberry, spindle tree and styrax and so on.

I have tried to cover the points you need to consider in making your selection under Seasonal Care and subject evaluation in the discussion of the species in Part II.

Check the soil and look at its composition. Is it pure akadama, an akadama-based mix or river sand and a light organic compost? Remember to look for buried roots. If it is in river sand, the tree probably came from the Nagoya area, and I always found these to be strongest. Trees from the region around Nagoya are often styled as Informal Upright with whorled branches. The branches are nicely shaped in downswept curves with uptilted terminals, like a

lazy-S shape. Check the bark formation and, while you are at it, look on the undersides of twigs and leaves for any escapee bugs or crawlers that have survived the Japanese exit fumigation process. On the trunks look for holes, about the diameter of a .45 bullet, indicating the presence of longhorn beetles. These are normally exit holes, but they are an indicator. Look for 'shotgun holes', about the diameter of a lead pellet, and for sawdust, which indicate borers.

Azaleas may have galls and some bud blast. Sometimes azaleas and firethorns have some leaf scorching on arrival, because the fumigation has dried the plants' tissues. All these things are treatable, so go ahead!

Fast-grown Bonsai

These are a lot of fun. They are easily developed and quickly thicken up when they are grown in the ground. This is the way a lot of bonsai are raised in Japan, and when they are well done, the results are excellent. All propagated material, nursery stock and skinny trunked bonsai can be developed in open growth.

The first step is to prepare an area in the garden or field by cultivating and fertilizing it well the year before it is to be used. This way the ground is in good condition and the fertilizer in the soil will have broken down.

Spring is the best time to undertake the next step. Take the material to the site with a tool kit. Prepare the roots by combing, spreading and lightly pruning them. Scoop shallow depressions in the soil to take the root mass. Have some wall tiles, old plates, old building blocks or something similar on hand and, as you plant, slide one of these under each trunk. This forces the roots sideways, and you must take care to spread them well because the side growth activity fattens the trunk.

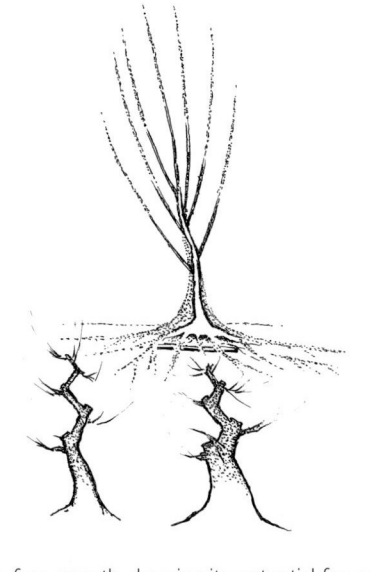

The tree in free growth, showing its potential for expansion.

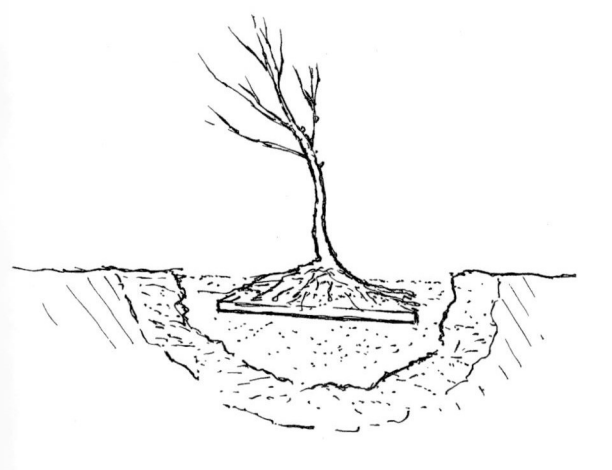

Preparing the material for fast-grown bonsai.

Water the plants in well. Leave for a month for the roots to recover, then feed the trees with Miracle-Gro or something similar to encourage growth. Feed every two weeks from mid-spring to early summer. From midsummer to early autumn feed once a month with 0–10–10.

Let top growth rocket away in six-week spurts. This builds wood. Shear the trees back to keep them in a roughly conical form. It is best to de-sucker azaleas and quince with their base dominance every time they throw strong basal shoots, unless you have a Group shape in mind.

Most plants will have a lot of heavy branch growth high up on the extending trunk line. These are natural alternative leaders, and as you cut back plants for the first time, make sure that you reduce their number. If more than about three are kept,

The evolution of the tree: the grow and chop system.

you can easily get reverse taper with the weight of top growth. The natural leader is trimmed at this time, and one of the companion branches should be chosen as a replacement. This creates a line that changes direction and is less thick than the old leader. New growth is cut back twice a year – and there you have the stepped-trunk taper system!

The system is repeated annually, and the trees are transplanted every third spring. Always spread and place a spreader tile under the roots. Carry on trunk fattening until the plant reaches the desired degree of tapered thickness.

If you are going for a big, heavy trunk, you can leave growth unpruned and the tree undisturbed for a couple of years or more. By this time, you will need to saw the trunk. Replacement growth will need almost the same development period to avoid skinny trunk steps. Gradually reduce the timing between cuts and the height allowed between each, and you will regain taper as you establish smaller and finer changes of trunk direction.

The alternative fast-grow method is to use a large grow box instead of open growth. The techniques are the same. The box is mobile – to an extent – and you can place it in a plastic greenhouse to force growth.

The branches on most species are more quickly developed than the trunk. It saves a lot of effort if these are grown after the trunk has thickened. The type of extended growth necessary to thicken the trunk is very coarse and is best cut away. Once the trunk is developed, you can take your time and build branches that really add to the character and structure of the new trunk. The choice is basically between sweeping, graceful lines and a stocky and contoured outline depending on how the proportions of your new trunk work out. If you still think the trunk needs more thickness, you will know what to do!

The styling I described as coming from Nagoya (see page 38) works well for branch shaping. In general terms, you are retaining most of the branches and are placing main and side branches so that they flow with the trunk movement.

Form the contours by pruning and wiring.

Periodic thinning simplifies the lines.

Branches are typically wired with, probably, 2mm ($\frac{1}{16}$ in) aluminium wire and the side branches with 1–1.5mm ($\frac{1}{32}$ in) wire. Again, branches are curved gently downwards at the trunk and uptilted at the terminal, like a lazy-S shape. They are formed using the same principle as that of trunk development, but there is one significant difference: the initial 5cm (2in) branch section is wired early as it extends. As the branch fattens and the wires look ready to bite, they are cut back to the wired zone, de-wired and the process is then followed with the

Branches are trained so that they angle away downwards from trunk movements. This trunk is compact, so the branches echo that feeling.

subsequent shooting of side buds. Like the trunk extension, this procedure is repeated twice a year.

This creates a series of short, characterful branches. They are treated in the same way each year and this builds branches at the rate of 5cm (2in) a year. There is, of course, more to it than just that: some buds are allowed some vertical extension before wiring and pruning and this, when repeated often enough, gives the domed section to the branch profile. In addition, the main branch lines should be curved laterally and all curves should vary. No two trees are ever quite the same because the branch rhythms echo those of the trunk. The branch/trunk echo arrangement is a system that works. Use it and all your trees will be really individual!

This trunk is a mix of short, abrupt and longer, slow curves. The branches echo and extend the structure and create mood in the design.

Rhododendron 'Blue Diamond'.

PART II

The Species

THIS SECTION OF THE BOOK
DESCRIBES TEN SPECIES OF FLOWERING
BONSAI AND EXPLAINS IN DETAIL
THEIR DAILY CARE.

Japanese Flowering Apricot

The Japanese flowering apricot *(Prunus mume)* is a wonderful plant to grow as a bonsai. It flowers on bare green wood, and both buds and the open flowers are fresh and clean cut. There is an almond fragrance that can scent a room when the tree is brought in for viewing, and the white, pink or red flowers, that are produced when the weather is still cold and warm days seem a long way off, give a feeling of spring. The bark develops and becomes thick with age. The trunk thickens well and darkens and contrasts well with the bright flowers. It is a beautiful tree, but what are the snags in growing it?

It is brittle. This means that you need to be extra careful when you wire it and begin to shape it. I use my hands like a clamp when I bend brittle wood. The method is to overlap your hands so that no part of the area to be bent is unsupported. Then close your hands and make a fist, pressing onto the wood. Squeeze and bend simultaneously and the wood will not break. The most effective wiring is done on new wood, but even that is brittle, so use the 'clamp'.

Water and feed – most growers underdo both – and be generous. If the weather is very hot or very

The flowers of *Prunus mume* 'Alba', a white-flowered apricot.

cold protect the tree. Do not let sun or frost dry out the wood, which can easily happen.

Apricot has close-grained wood, which lends itself to carving. Old bonsai of this species are often developed from rotted-out stumps, and to hollow or carve the trunk is to emulate that same visual characteristic. The key is not to overdo the carving, from the standpoints of both plant health and aesthetics. If you are going to embark on a heavy carving programme, rest the tree by breaking your schedule into at least two sessions separated by recuperative months. And when you are carving, make sure it really 'works' with the grain of the wood. If the texture is wrong, the illusion is lost. I like to tint the newly carved wood of any tree by applying a little gouache water-colour paint. This dulls down the 'attacked by human' look and refines the texture.

Choose a container with care. Too many apricots are planted in an 'export blue' pot – 'export blue' is my name for that cheap, shiny and unrelieved blue that is made in the East for the Western market. It does the least for any bonsai. Instead, select a muted, semi-matt glaze in off-white, muddy-yellow, slate blue or celadon green. Unglazed ware works, too. Brown, dull red, grey and black are good combined with the features of this tree. The apricot as bonsai can suggest an ancient orchard tree or some weathered mountain plant, and the pot is the final element in creating this image.

Seasonal Care

Training Styles Informal Upright, Leaning, Semi-cascade, Cascade, Literati, Driftwood, Root over Rock, Tree on Rock, Raft, Root-connected, Group.

Likely Source Apricots are readily available as imported Japanese bonsai and possibly also from local nursery stock.

Propagation It is easy to propagate from cuttings taken in autumn and stored over winter in damp sand and inserted in spring. The apricot is also easy to graft and easy to layer.

Type and Description A deciduous, flowering, small tree.

Habitat China, Korea and Japan.

Trunk Young shoots are green and the bark ages to buff-grey. The inner bark is wine coloured.

Foliage The leaves are typical *Prunus* form: spear-shaped and deep green. The growth terminals are reddish.

Flowers Flowers are borne on bare wood from late winter to early spring, according to variety. Most varieties are single-flowered, but there are double forms. The buds and open flowers together are a beautiful sight. The flowers are almond scented.

Cultivars There are many cultivars. Commonly available are 'Alba' – single white flowers; 'Alboplena' – semi-double white flowers; 'Alphandii' – semi-double pink flowers; 'Beni-shidon' – double red flowers.

Soil Two parts weathered sand, three parts oak leaf mould/mulch, three parts composted peat and two parts compost or akadama give a rich but well-drained soil.

Potting and Repotting When potting and repotting, use medium or deeper containers because this tree likes cool roots. Root-prune younger plants every year and older trees every other year or less often, according to age and vigour. Root-prune after flowering, which is usually early spring in temperate zones.

Water Keep damp at all times; the apricot requires plenty of water.

Feeding After flowering, feed every two weeks until midsummer with half-strength Miracid. During summer and until autumn use 0–10–10 every two weeks, diluted at a rate of 15g to 4.5 litres (1 tablespoon to a gallon) of water. Dose the tree with Trace Element Frit every year.

Trimming Shorten branches after flowering, cutting above an outward-facing bud, but be careful that you do not cut too close. Let new growth grow unchecked. In autumn shorten branches again, enough to restore the shape but not so close as to cut off the flowers. The flower buds show up as bigger and fatter at this time. You should thin out to refine the shape.

Note: one year in three, cut new growth back to two leaves. This keeps branches leafy. They can otherwise over-flower and die back. Older branches are pruned after flowering.

Wiring Wire in early summer and de-wire by autumn. Use aluminium wire.

Position The apricot likes bright sun but do not let it get it too hot. Keep out of frost.

Pests and Diseases Aphids may be present, but the plant is largely trouble free. Peach leaf curl should be treated with lime sulphur as a pre-emergent spray; Bordeaux mixture also works.

Material Type

The two most likely types of material are imported Japanese bonsai in a range of sizes and, less frequently, normal nursery stock. I ordered some from a large nursery in Britain, and they turned out to be delightful plants. They were the variety 'Beni-shidon', which bears bright carmine-red, almond-scented flowers.

Container-grown Nursery Stock The shapes most likely suggested by the nursery stock are the Informal Upright, Twin-trunk and Driftwood. All these are achieved, initially, by trunk reduction with a saw. Good nursery stock for landscaping is often 2.4–3m (8–10ft) tall and with a base trunk diameter of up to 8cm (3in). *Prunus cerasifera* Myrobalan Group, often used as an understock for the strong trunk and roots it produces, is good for bonsai on its own, and it bears masses of small white flowers.

> **You will need:** rake, saw, shears, jin pliers, potting soil, large prepared container.
> **Season:** late winter to early spring.

Remove the tree from the pot and assess your material for trunk movement, diameter and surface roots. The bottom 60cm (2ft) of the trunk are what counts. Look for a trunk that will sit well with a nucleus of usable surface roots. Use the rake to comb away the soil around the base so that you can see the lines.

Study the trunk from all angles and look for more than one pleasing aspect. Bonsai are three-dimensional, and if you can find a way to combine the many features that most trees offer, your design will immediately be full and visually satisfying.

Equally, if your tree does not offer this, move on to one that does. You should look for an upper branch that will work as a replacement leader with the trunk when it is shortened. When you have found this, saw the trunk down, making a diagonal cut. Do not cut too close to the new leader because apricots are prone to drying up and die-back. You will need to seal the cut carefully.

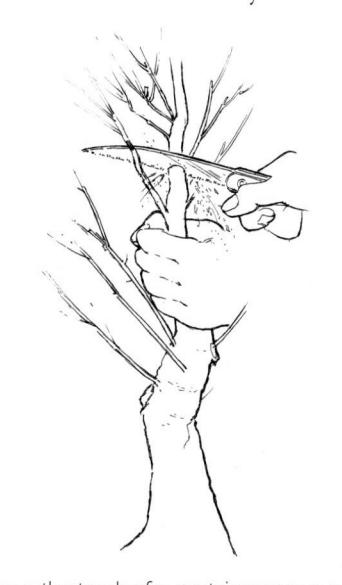

Cutting down the trunk of a container-grown nursery stock of Japanese flowering apricot.

Check the main branches for inner branch lines that can take over once the terminals are reduced. This works in the same way as the trunk shortening. Shorten all branches that are to be in the permanent framework of the design. Remove all others completely and seal all cuts.

Clear the root area.

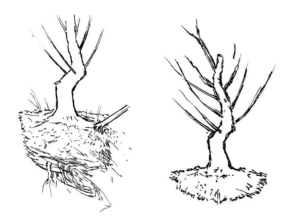

Left: root-prune to remove heavy roots. **Right:** the apricot after root pruning.

Return to the roots and remove the taproot and any heavy lower roots. Comb out and reduce the root mass and prune it to even it. You are looking for root fibre, and cutting back promotes finer roots. Spread out the roots radially so that the surface roots really do support the tree, and check the root mass for size in the container. Make sure there is a good drainage course of shingle, 12mm ($\frac{1}{2}$ in) deep, and a good layer of the suggested soil mix (see page 15). Set the tree on the soil and wriggle it to settle it in, before topping up with more soil. You will probably need to criss-cross tie the trunk to the container. If

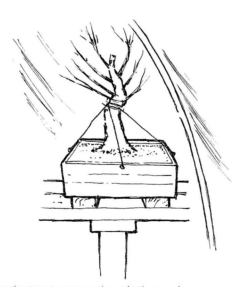

Leave the tree to recover in a plastic greenhouse.

you are using a wooden box, screw eyes are useful location points. Make sure that the trunk is steady, then place the apricot in a plastic greenhouse (poly-tunnel) and water in well.

Let the tree sprout freely and grow strongly for a season. If you attend to watering and feeding, the tree will settle well. Shorten new growth in autumn, after you can see the flower buds. Leave it for a while so you will have a lot of bloom. That completes year 1. The biggest mistake you can make with an apricot is to style straightaway. That year in which the tree is left to settle ensures a good future.

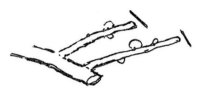

Year 2: shorten growth above flower buds.

You can plant out those trees that were set aside from the first trunk selection and use them as stock plants for cuttings and layers.

After flowering, remove the flowers and check for leaf buds.

In year 2, after you have enjoyed the crop of flowers, cut the overgrown branches short, above outward-facing buds.

Remove all spent flowers completely and check to see you have left two or three leaf buds on the shortened shoot. Growth is now left to push strongly and may be tip-pinched when it has extended to six or seven leaves.

Pruning and wiring make believable branch forms.

New growth is wired in late spring.

The apricot after three or four years.

Wire the new growth into position in late spring. Use aluminium wire and bend very carefully. Branches are curved downwards and are an exception to the lazy-S principle, in which a shallow, downswept curve is answered by an upturn, terminating the shape. The reason for this simple arc arrangement is that new shoots rocket vertically, and by shortening them in autumn and wiring new growth the following spring, a mixture of shallow curves and short straight lines is formed, which follows the natural habit of the apricot. This process sets up the shape pretty quickly.

Imported Japanese Bonsai You can buy imported trees at any stage of development. Most importers do not know the names of the varieties involved, or, even if they do, they are just copied from the name tags on the trees as they come into the country.

You will need: rake, saw, shears, jin pliers, potting soil, large prepared container, router for carving driftwood.
Season: late winter.

Check the roots. These are often shortened right back before export, and if the importer has used heavy akadama to pot the tree up, the emerging roots will probably suffocate. Gently wiggle the tree in the soil and check near the trunk – you are looking for a crack in the soil circling close in to the trunk. If you see it, the tree has been chopped. Buy the tree in early spring, enjoy the flowers, then wash off the soil and use the suggested lighter mixture and all should be well. Greenhouse protection after this operation will help. Grow the tree on, following the notes under Seasonal Care (see pages 44–5).

The most common shapes for apricots at the bonsai nursery are the Informal Upright, but also sometimes Literati, Twin-trunk and miniature bonsai. Check the small bonsai for vine weevil. While I was visiting a large European nursery I found that in an average matchbox-sized pot there were about three of the larvae.

Sometimes you find a supposed 'specimen' apricot with a lot of dead lower branches. It will be

An imported Japanese bonsai – neglected stock with dead lower branches.

growing in heavy soil, of course. If it is possible to negotiate a good price, buy it, because with care you can make good Literati and Driftwood shapes.

First, loosen the soil. Check the roots for any damage and wash them off. Use the right soil mixture and a large, well-drained pot. Place the tree in a plastic greenhouse (poly-tunnel) and spoil it with water and feed for a season. In a year or so, or whenever the tree has obviously recovered and feels firm in the pot, you can consider converting it to the new shape, which you should undertake in late winter.

Plan your tree. Use an electric chain saw or router (depending on the size of the trunk) to begin carving the trunk. Follow the natural grain of the wood and respect the live bark outside the carved area. You may want to cover the bark with tape to protect it. Routers have great torque and kick sideways unless they are very firmly held.

Dan Robinson advocates bolting another handle through the hole located near the nose of most chain saws for fine control. This makes an incredible difference to the handling feel of the

Some dead branches are made into jin.

saw, which becomes 100 per cent easier to use. If you use the saw, refine the carving later with a router. You will need to allow drying time for fine

Where large branches have died, the stumps can be hollowed.

The front view of an old apricot.

The back view of the same apricot.

Left: an acceptable Literati created from another damaged tree. **Right:** the original trunk, after carving and recovery time, has been repotted and wired.

detailing the wood. The original dead branches can become part of the design either as jin or *uro* branches or hollows. Do not hurry the job: enjoy each stage.

After styling, put the tree back in the greenhouse for a year off with plenty of water and feeding.

Bonsai Re-creation

The Japanese flowering apricot shown opposite and above was imported from Japan as an old specimen in the late 1960s or early 1970s. It is being re-grown after suffering some die-back, which is why the trunk and branches appear a little unresolved.
HEIGHT: 60cm (24in); trunk diameter: 8cm (3in); AGE: about 50 years; flowers: white.

Trunk The quality of the trunk is very fine. There was originally an excellent taper, and this is still present on the tall, dead portion of the trunk. The tree was probably a collected plant. There are good indications of this in the *uro* hollows, which appear entirely consistent with natural damage.

A close-up of the trunk texture.

The trunk grew slowly in the first instance, as can be seen in the tapered line. The rough bark, whose formation is largely uninterrupted, is another indication of slow evolution.

TRUNK RECONSTRUCTION Such a trunk can be reproduced if it is fast grown and tapered by the

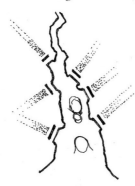

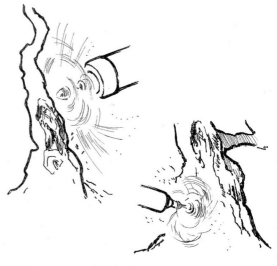

The trunk form is re-created using the fast-grown, stepped-taper methods.

Left: the stumps caused by the taper steps are smoothed or scooped out with a router. **Right:** *Uro* hollows are added with a Makita die-grinder.

of bark on this tree is wonderful, but even this can be hurried a little, by scarring the bark superficially to hasten the natural plating process.

Roots These are well distributed and have a really settled look. Their formation adds quality to the trunk, and there is a lot of bark texture present.

ROOT RECONSTRUCTION The roots can be worked on and spread and surfaced at each repotting. I discovered one way to enhance the roots by accident. If you keep the tree in a compact container for a while, without disturbing the surface roots, the roots fatten up and become prominent when the tree is fed and watered freely. As long as repotting is carried out, without moving the top roots too much, the tree can stay in the container without any detrimental effects. When you do move it into something bigger, leave

stepped method. If the scar damage is carefully carved, detailed, painted and left with the grain open, the weathering process will give a lot of the same texture. The bark will age at the natural rate. The aged texture

The bark is sliced a little to hasten the formation of bark platelets.

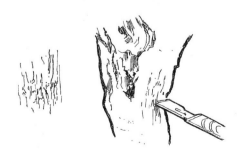

The tree in bloom.

the lines of the root nucleus undisturbed and you will have pretty much created the size and shape of the old root system shown here.

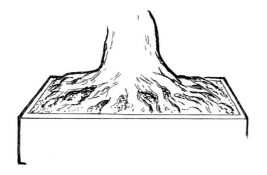

Roots are developed into thick forms by keeping the tree initially in a small pot.

Branches These are pleasantly shaped but they are new and easily produced.

Overall Shape The dead trunk is the key to the real success of this design. Whether it is retained or removed, each trunk presents great possibilities for radical improvement, provided that the manner used agrees with the identity of the plant.

The overall shape with the dead trunk retained. The trunk is carved and thinned using a router. It is tint-painted as described in the section on Trunk Carving (see pages 18–19). The foliage pad at top left is removed, and it is potted in a smaller, deeper pot with a striking glaze.

DEAD TRUNK RETAINED If the line is kept it needs to be reduced so that it works better with the emerging branch–trunk structure. This is probably best done by carving to thin the old line and emphasize the new, vigorous re-grown appearance of an old recovering tree.

DEAD TRUNK REMOVED If the trunk is removed, a couple of possibilities suggest themselves. First, why not remove the top left-hand portion of the live canopy as well? This would do great things for the geometry of the trunk. The second possibility is to retain a stubby portion of the dead trunk and to carve it down, continuing the carving into the lower trunk. This would provide a more flowing line. Another possibility is to reduce the whole branch structure and keep it really small, so that the trunk appears enormous. There are so many things you can do with such a nice trunk.

Whichever solution is adopted, the pot is wrong: it is too young for the old bark.

Left: the overall shape with the dead trunk removed except for a stubby portion. The stump is carved and this is carried into the lower trunk. The pot has more angles and depth.
Right: the whole trunk is retained, but its thickness is reduced and the length of the branch area is made really small. The tree is placed in a small square pot.

Japanese Satsuki and Kurume Azaleas

A Kurume azalea.

Most of the Japanese azaleas (*Rhododendron indicum* and *R. obtusum*) are very successful as bonsai. Even ancient plants produce their brilliant flowers with all the freshness of a young nursery plant. Though essentially shrubs, these plants can be grown in the image of a tree, with a single well-defined trunk, and they can be encouraged to produce massive surface roots. Most of the group have compact, dark green foliage that lends itself to shaping, and the plants accept pruning well and respond strongly. The trunks become fissured and the bark thickens with age.

The flowers are glorious and can alone be sufficient reason to grow these plants. There are untold numbers of Satsuki azaleas (*R. indicum*), which are constantly hybridized in Japan and which are classified by the shape, size and colour pattern of the flowers. The Kurume azaleas (*R. obtusum*), too, have wonderful flowers, but they are usually smaller and in solid colours. The smaller flowers have a more refined appearance.

Beautiful plants and with not too many problems either – it sounds too good to be true. But they really are easy, provided you give them a few basics and 'keep it coming'. Azaleas need a light, acidic soil and a good reservoir of moisture underneath. The soil really needs to be light and spongy. The reservoir action in this case does not mean using deep pots; rather, the pots must be wide enough to accommodate the spread under a fair bit of the branch pattern. Azaleas have fine, shallow roots, and they like to spread them. Branches and, therefore, the whole tree do better if they largely under-pinned by the root pattern. Think of it as a mirror image, above and below the soil.

Azaleas are very brittle. Be very careful when you wire that you do not break the branches.

Use the suggested feeds and follow the schedule. Azaleas use a lot of energy in flower production and need help. Always make sure you are feeding on damp soil and never on dry.

Remember when you are pruning that these plants are base dominant. Maintain a balance with the strong lower areas if you are pruning the higher zones. Do keep azaleas damp and in dappled shade. If the fine roots in hot, dry soil are exposed to strong sun, you can expect some damage, even die-back, with a lot of the more sensitive varieties. Spray the leaves in the growing season and when not in flower. Azaleas are largely from woodland origins and like these conditions.

Do deadhead. I know it is a chore, but the seeds that are produced do run the plant down, quite apart from robbing you of flower for next year.

Choose an appropriate container. With all that riot of colour to contend with, it is better to understate the pot. Muted tones in glazed ware in off-white, muddy-yellow, dull blue and green or unglazed ware in brown and grey will complement these beautiful plants.

Seasonal Care

Training Styles Informal, Leaning, Semi-cascade, Cascade, Literati, Root over Rock, Tree on Rock, Twin-trunk, Raft, Root-Connected, Group.
Likely Source Azaleas are readily available as imported Japanese bonsai, at specialist retailers and as local nursery stock.
Propagation They can be easily propagated from cuttings or by divisions or layering.

Type and Description An evergreen flowering shrub.
Habitat Japan.
Trunk Young shoots are pale green. The bark ages to buff and dark brown.
Foliage The leaves are spear shaped and glossy dark green. They range, according to variety, in size and length from 1cm ($\frac{1}{2}$ in) to 2.5cm (1in).
Flowers Flowers are so profusely borne that the leaves are often hidden. Flowering season is in mid- to late spring.

The flowers of Satsuki azaleas are usually 2.5–5cm (1–2in) across, with pointed or round petals. Flower colours are diverse and there are zoned, margined, threaded, striped, spotted and single colour forms. The flowers of Kurume azaleas are small, about 1cm ($\frac{1}{2}$ in) across. Most flowers are single but there are 'hose-in-hose' types (flowers one inside the other).
Cultivars Commonly available and strong (not all are) Satsuki cultivars include: 'Eikan' – round petals, frilled, white, pink and striped; 'Korin' – pointed petals, deep pink red; 'Osakasuki' – round petals, deep pink.

Azalea flowers.

Frost-rimed leaves.

Kurume varieties commonly available are: 'Hinode-giri'– crimson-purple flowers; 'Hino-mayo' – pink flowers; 'Kure-no-yuki' – white, hose-in-hose flowers. All these have typical, neat azalea flowers.

Soil Use a mix of six parts composted peat, two parts akadama and two parts oak leaf mould.

Potting and Repotting Root-prune and pot up after flowering is finished. Younger azaleas are repotted annually and older plants every other year or even less, according to age.

Water Keep azaleas damp and spray foliage except when in flower.

Feeding Feed in spring when shoot activity starts until early summer, then change to 0–10–10 every two weeks. In midsummer feed with Miracid, then change back to 0–10–10 every two weeks from late summer. Stop feeding by early autumn. Dose the tree with Trace Element Frit once a year.

Note: always feed azaleas at half strength.

Trimming Prune unwanted branches in early spring. Pinch soft new growth back to increase density. Do not pinch after early summer or flowers will not form. Pinch off dangling leaves and inner growth that gets too dense. Always deadhead old flowers.

Note: this plant is base dominant, so if you prune the apex, remember to preserve the balance of vigour by also pruning the lower branches.

Wiring Wire after flowering is over. Use aluminium wire and de-wire by autumn. Every part of the azalea is brittle.

Position Azaleas need to be in good light, but do not let the plants get baked. They like dappled shade. Keep out of frost.

Pests and Diseases Bud blast can be a problem. A brown discoloration appears over autumn/winter and buds go dark. Treat by removing affected buds

A small Kurume azalea.

and by spraying with a fungicide such as Zineb or Bordeaux mixture. The condition is spread by insects so spray with mild insecticide.

Rhododendron gall is seen in small, uneven swollen areas, like pinkish-white water blisters, on leaves, buds and flowers. Treat by cutting away affected parts and isolate infected plants to lessen spread by insect contact.

Material Type

The most likely sources of plants will be imported Japanese bonsai, in a range of sizes, or container-grown stock available at specialized nurseries. General nurseries and garden centres sometimes carry good azaleas.

Container-grown Nursery Stock These are usually bushy because nurserymen pinch out single stem propagation to encourage the shape. You will find a lot of multi-stemmed plants, some of them demanding to be Raft or Root-connected bonsai. The other forms these plants suggest are Semi-cascade and Cascade. You will also find Literati and Twin-trunk among the less spreading and more upright plants.

The best kind of material to find is that which has hung around a bit in the nursery and has had a chance to thicken up. Make sure that the plants have not dried up while they were left on the nursery shelves: check for leaf scorch and a lot of dead twigs, which are the tell-tale signs of drought. If you do find damage, try and assess how much. If no more than a third of the plant appears damaged, it is probably worth the risk. Mostly azaleas come back pretty well if you follow the suggestions for position and feeding under Seasonal Care (see page 55). Not all older material has been left over, however; you may find recycled stock plants, and these are very desirable.

You will need: turntable, shears, long-handled trimming shears, fine scissors, branch cutters, root cutters, scalpel, probe stick, rake, prepared containers or boxes with tie strings, wound sealant. **Season:** choose azaleas in flower, normally mid- to late spring; they are styled after flowering.

All styling requires a lot of foliage reduction, so as you pick the plants with flowers you like, look for the trunk lines, too. Try to imagine the trunk as a central line without branches and see what form comes to mind. It is useful to have one of the shapes in mind, but you do not have to make the tree conform to some predetermined matrix. The shapes listed above happen to suit the plants and are commonly found in nursery stock, but if you find an interesting trunk line that seems totally unorthodox and you like it, then buy it!

I have always found that once you think of a bonsai as a sculpture rather than a formula, it lifts your thinking into a broader and more imaginative spectrum. What matters is the overall form and the trunk and branches working together in a unified and attractive shape.

A close-up of the flowers of a Kurume azalea.

Take your azalea and place it on the turntable at a comfortable working height. Turn and examine all sides of the trunk or trunks. If you are going for a Raft or Root-connected shape, you can begin by thinning out the multi-stemmed growth. Look for lines that make a harmony of form when viewed, first, as simple masses and then with their supporting trunk structures. You are looking for clouds of foliage at differing heights on a series of trunks of different weights. When you have selected the trunks, clear the base of other shoots. Always seal all cuts.

Assessing the form of a container-grown nursery azalea.

Left: a Raft trunk is formed from a keeled-over planting angle. **Right:** place the plant sideways and assess it for well-placed 'trunks'. Prune the other branches.

Raft The true Raft has a recumbent main trunk, and you can often find this in container-grown stock when the trunk has been allowed to tip over sideways in the container and has re-rooted along the buried area. It is a simple matter to create a Raft. Simply take the plant out of the pot and wash off and separate the roots until they can be spread out flat. Remove all branches on the side of the trunk that is to face downwards, then use a scalpel to cut windows in the bark adjacent to the pruned branches and peel away the bark. Treat the windows with rooting hormone.

The thinned-out Raft, with the lower branches pruned.

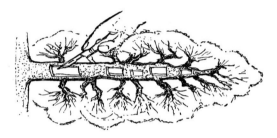

Cut windows in the bark.

Gently unravel the roots. Azaleas are densely rooted, and it is easier to use a probe stick such as a garden cane, wooden knitting needle or chopstick. The probe removes soil clods by passing between the roots without tearing them.

Take one of the prepared containers, half-filled with the suggested soil mix (see page 55) and spread a little chopped sphagnum moss over the soil. This acts as a reservoir when the azalea is re-rooting.

Lay the azalea down in the prepared container and spread the roots. Flatten the upper half of the rootball as far as possible and spread the lower half

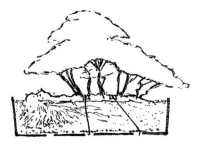

Prune the existing roots and place the flat when potting up the azalea.

beside and below the horizontal trunk line. When you are happy with the roots, sift more soil in and level it at the midway line along the horizontal trunk. Do not cover the Raft trunk, but you will probably have to mound the soil over the upper half of the old rootball.

Tie the trunk down to immobilize it, using friction pads where the strings cross. Rubber or plastic tubing is good for this, and you can slide the string through it so it will not move. Place the plant in a plastic greenhouse (poly-tunnel) and water well with a fine spray. Delay further soil watering until it feels damp rather than soggy and then try to maintain that condition. Spray the leaves periodically.

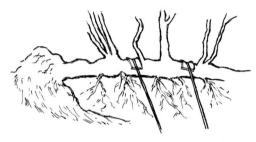

Roots will appear around the windows in the bark.

Results vary with the age of the wood, but you should have side roots along the trunk in a month or so. By the end of the year you will probably have side roots that are of matchstick thickness. Keep them damp. Moist roots fatten. You can even add a pad of damp sphagnum moss to each side of the trunk to maintain moisture. You can thin out the branches to improve the proportions of the planting, but let the foliage grow strongly first so that it can recover from the initial thinning to set up the trunks and foliage pads.

The original root is much reduced at the next repotting.

Repot the azalea in year 3 and check the development of the new root system. Depending on how much you find, you either reduce the old root mass or remove it altogether. It is usually safer to reduce it a lot but to delay the final removal until the next time the azalea is repotted. You can certainly use a better container now.

Root-connected Root-connected trees are handled in a very similar way to the Raft style. The main difference is the use of the root conglomeration as the base rather than the trunk.

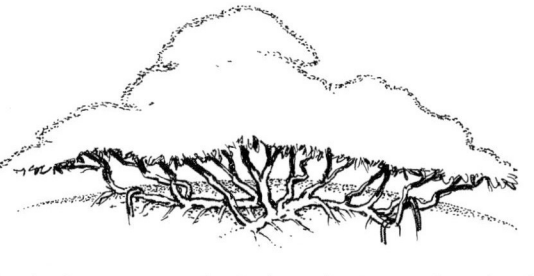

For the Root-connected style the azalea is transplanted and outer lines are pegged down for additional rooting. It is then treated in the same way as the Raft.

After the initial trunk and branch thinning, the roots are opened up and carefully separated and spread. There will be a lot of upper roots and basal trunk suckers mixed up together. Place the plant on the turntable and spin it slowly around, assessing where the best combinations of branch–trunk lines occur. The outlying branches and trunks are usually already rooted after being buried in mulch. They can be pegged down to give extra spread and variation to the rising trunk lines.

Set the azalea in the prepared container, proceeding as for the Raft, with the pot half filled with soil and top dressed with moss. Spread the roots! When you are happy with the location and angle of the planting, sift more soil around the roots, making sure you leave no air pockets. Gently use the probe stick to search for holes and add soil as necessary. Leave just the crests of the connecting root lines exposed. Tie in the trunk as for the Raft and all subsequent steps are identical. Seal all cuts.

In year 2, with both Raft and Root-connected trees, new growth is allowed to grow long and is trimmed back and wired. Side buds sprout and are allowed to grow long before they, too, are trimmed and wired. This process orders and shapes the design. If you want flowers, do not trim growth after the end of early summer.

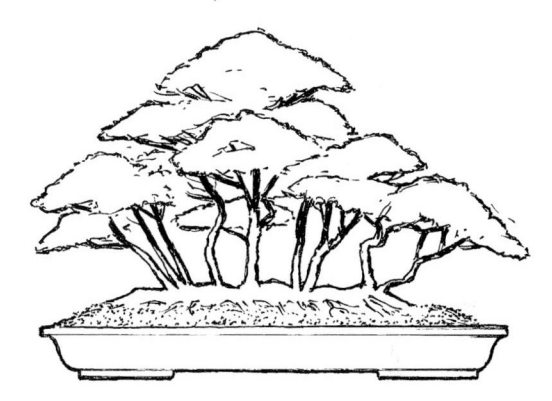

The branches of both Raft and Root-connected plants are thinned after flowering.

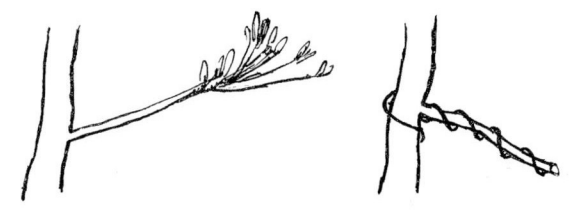

Left: shoots are allowed to grow freely. **Right:** the branch is trimmed and wired.

Side shoots are allowed to grow and get strong.

A pruned and wired branch, with new shoots developing.

The branch structure after wiring.

When repotting in year 3, carefully remove the soil between root laterals with a probe stick. Trim wedges of dense roots away *or* shorten the side roots this time and wedge-prune next time.

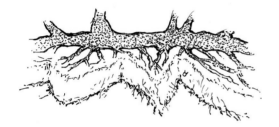

During repotting take out wedges of roots.

Thin the depth of soil.

Thin out the lower roots and pick out about half of the old soil. This allows for fresh soil to penetrate the root system and encourages strong growth. Next time remove the other half of the old soil.

The settled shape. The structure thickens and looks convincing.

The tree will now settle and grow strongly, and trunks, branches and roots will thicken. Periodic thinning will keep the shape light and airy. Maintain the shape with trimming and wiring, and within five years you will have a great tree.

Imported Bonsai Visit the nursery and pick your azalea when it is in flower. If you choose a tree in the year it was imported, it will be nice and compact. However, if it has been around for a while, it will probably be overgrown. The Informal Upright is by far the most often seen shape. Enjoy the flowers while they last.

An imported Satsuki azalea bonsai with neglected branches.

Any stumps left on the trunk from fast trunk development in the field can be carved now. They can either be carefully carved flat and sealed, or they can be carved out as trunk hollows to suit the mood of the tree. Some azalea trunks can be quite knotted and gnarled, and hollows can fit in very well. Seal the edges of carved areas to stop the bark drying up.

The stumps left from field growing are treated and the basic branch profiles are tidied up.

A bonsai rhododendron of the Blue Diamond Group, photographed in 1996.

lessens transplant shock. When the roots have been cleaned, trimmed and spread out, you can pot up the azalea in a new container and be confident that the tree will thicken up and be vigorous.

Maintain standard aftercare, and keep the branches vigorous by thinning, growing on and cutting back. Enjoy your tree as it matures into a finely shaped bonsai. The flowers and leaves of the azalea are very interesting.

Bonsai Re-creation

The grower has adapted this hybrid azalea of the Blue Diamond Group from a plant bought in a garden centre. The natural lines of the trunk and the first branch on the right have been skilfully used to set the mood of the tree. The plant has a very tree-like, natural feeling. There is a lot of movement in the trunk, branches and root display.

HEIGHT: 56cm (22in); trunk diameter: 5cm (2in); AGE: about 15 years; flowers: lavender.

After the azalea's health has been built up by a change of soil and by adequate feeding and watering, it is responding to pruning by filling out and developing well.

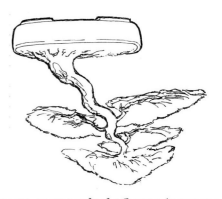

Thin the branches out and wire them so that the shape blends with each trunk direction rather than acting against it. Repot the tree and pick away at the old soil with the soil probe. Recycling some of the old soil by adding a proportion to the new mix

Trunk Reconstruction Plants with suitable trunks are to be found if you spend time looking. This particular example could be reproduced from a cutting if you wished to follow the form absolutely.

The strength of the trunk lies in the way it flows from the well-defined root element to the

The trunk is chopped and a new apex is formed by pinching back the mass of new shoots.

The trunk line is extended and the apex developed from a mass of side branches.

The trunk has been developed by shaping a cutting.

thrusting right branch and then swings back left. The lower trunk is interesting, and a lot of the basal flare comes from the roots. If you look closely you can see lines in the bark indicating where roots coalesced and added to the trunk girth.

The pronounced curve in the trunk above the right branch is actually created by the branch base turning downwards before growing out. The negative space around the lower trunk is varied and interesting and the trunk line stands out boldly. The upper trunk, which is masked by branching, may be formed by pruning it short to make a crown from the mass of resulting shoots, or the trunk line may be extended and the same effect generated by training side branches.

Branch Reconstruction The branch forms are diverse and interesting. The lower right-hand branch is well formed and the grower has made excellent use of the natural rising growth pattern of the species. The cleaned main branch line is characterful and the 'knuckles' of the rising branches give an aged and structured look. The foliage line is convincing and natural.

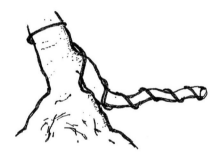

The lower right-hand branch is wired forwards, downwards and outwards and is then pruned.

The branch contours are grown by wiring selected shoots and pinching for additional budding.

There is good asymmetrical balance throughout the design, and the other branches have been styled to echo the lower right-hand one, largely placed by wiring. The lower right is a natural form that can be duplicated by pruning. The lower trunk is very strong and a base branch is quickly developed.

Root Reconstruction This root formation is often found on such dwarf azalea/rhododendron stock. The roots may be developed on a cutting by encouraging a good radial position and then by using a small container.

Plant the azalea so that it is slightly mounded, spread the roots and make sure that they flow smoothly into the soil, then cover them. After a couple of seasons they can be exposed a little by raising the plant.

The pot seen in the photographs is by Gordon Duffett. The simple elegance of the form harmonizes with the texture of the tree and the glaze complements the tree both in and out of flower.

A close-up of the flower.

The azalea flowers are a warm lavender colour.

Cotoneaster

The cotoneaster's red fruit.

The rockspray cotoneaster (*Cotoneaster horizontalis*) is a familiar plant that can be seen in most gardens, but it makes a great bonsai because all the features of the plant are in scale for bonsai purposes, whether it is 8cm (3in) or 58cm (23in) high. The flowers are small and the red berries are gorgeous when seen up close. The leaves change colour before falling, when they reveal the plant's compact frame.

Cotoneasters make excellent small-size bonsai in whatever style, but they really shine as rock-grown plants. They seem to belong with rocks.

They are very hardy and forgiving plants and accept training like a dream. Cotoneasters will, however, develop at an incredible rate if they are fed lushly with nitrogen, which has the effect of fattening not so much the trunk, where you want it, but rather the branch system, and as a result the plant loses scale. Keeping your plant on low nitrogen as suggested in the notes should take care of the problem. If the worst happens and your plant does get too heavy, you can always layer the offending portions and start them off as little plants in their own right.

Watering plays a major part in success with this species – they love it. If your plant is rock-grown or if it is a very small one, it will particularly appreciate a spray over its leaves in the evenings.

With pink-white flowers, red berries, green mosses and perhaps rocks to consider, the pot colour is important: a dark midnight blue, slate blue, muted yellow and off-white all contrast and work well. Informal pots – ovals and soft-cornered forms – all complement the plant. Avoid shiny glazes.

Seasonal Care

Training Styles Informal, Leaning, Wind-swept, Semi-cascade, Cascade, Literati, Root over Rock, Tree on Rock, Twin-trunk, Raft, Root-connected, Group.

Likely Sources Cotoneasters are readily available as garden plants, as imported Japanese bonsai and as local nursery stock.

Propagation Easy to propagate from cuttings or by division or layering.

Type and Description A deciduous, flowering and fruiting shrub.

Habitat China.

Trunk Young shoots are green. The bark ages to buff-silvery brown.

Foliage Small, rounded spear shape; the leaves turn bright red in autumn.

Flowers Small, pink-white flowers appear in mid- to late spring.

Fruit Berries appear as the flowers fade. They are green at first, becoming bright, shiny red by autumn.

Cultivars *Cotoneaster horizontalis* 'Variegatus' has cream-variegated leaves and pretty autumn colour.

Soil Three parts composted peat, two parts akadama, three parts leaf mould and two parts sand.

Potting and Repotting Younger plants are root-pruned annually, older plants every other year. Do this in early spring when the buds swell.

Water Keep cotoneasters evenly damp – they like water.

Feeding Feed when leaves swell until the flowering period, using half-strength Miracle-gro or a similar feed, every two weeks. Alternate with 0–10–10. After flowering, use fish emulsion instead of Miracle-Gro and resume alternate feeds until late summer. Do not feed in hot weather to avoid coarse growth. From late summer to mid-autumn feed every two weeks with 0–10–10. Dose the tree with Trace Element Frit once a year.

Trimming Branches can be pruned in early spring, and new shoots push in late spring. They can trimmed back to one pair of new leaves, extended or removed according to the design of the tree.

Wiring Wire new growth in early summer. Use aluminium wire. Older wood is hard – sometimes very hard – and may need cutting back to redirect growth rather than risking splits or breaks through the heavy pressure needed to bend it.

Position Cotoneasters need good light, but do not let them get baked in hot sun. Dappled light is best. Keep out of hard frost.

Pests Watch for scale insects and aphids and spray accordingly. An environmentally friendly spray, such as Volck (an oil-based product), will keep scale insects in check. Keep the plant dryish a day before and after spraying because the leaf surface is temporarily sealed.

Other Species Practically all cotoneasters make excellent bonsai, with the exception of some tree varieties, which are very coarse in texture.

Material Type

A lot of excellent material can be found growing right in the garden. *Cotoneaster horizontalis* is very common as a landscape plant but is used nowhere near enough for bonsai. Nursery stock and imported Japanese bonsai are other options, but there is nothing like finding and developing your own plant.

Whether you start with a garden or a nursery plant, you will need to establish it in a large pot and let it grow freely for a year or so. The plant grows as an arched multi-stemmed fan and becomes a mass of lines. The curving habit is attractive and easy to work with as bonsai and suggests a Cascade or Semi-cascade form.

You will need: shears, long-handled trimming shears, branch cutters, rake, turntable, wire cutters, aluminium training wire and wound sealant.
Season: early spring, as buds swell.

Begin by searching the plant for good trunk lines. The average clump of rockspray cotoneaster will have at least a couple of usable forms if you study it carefully. Put it on a turntable and slowly rotate the plant. Look for lines that can either make the full-length shape or may continue their line if a side branch is used.

The concept.

Remove growth that falls below the line of the future branches and remove all side growths that spring from branch bases.

Container-grown nursery stock of *Cotoneaster horizontalis*.

Remove all competing trunk lines. Use branch cutters and cut close. Clean up the root base and check for surface roots. There is often something worth looking at below the congested mess of dead leaves, layered trunks and main root base. Surfaced roots are a bonus with the Cascade forms because they steady the shape visually and physically.

Opposite twigs and junctions are thinned.

Cotoneaster horizontalis is brittle, and the wood splits easily at branch forks. Assess the trunk line and decide if it is bendable by flexing it in the fingers. If cotoneaster wood has matured but is not thicker than a pencil, it will usually accept gentle, slow wire bending. If you want sharper bends, you would be better advised to cut back and re-grow the line. The green shoots are easily bent.

A typical resolution of the problem is to combine both factors and wire part way, choosing a minor, bendable side branch that can be wired into position to continue the line. Wire the trunk first, then the side branches. It is probably a good thing not to wire the thinnest growth at this season. Anything thinner than a matchstick is left to thicken and will be wired later. Using the 'clamp' technique (see pages 13–15), squeeze and bend the wood. Take it slowly and carefully.

As well as the major downward sweep, the trunk looks better if it curves laterally as well. Make the curves three-dimensional, not too much, but do avoid the flat S-form, which gets monotonous. Wire curve those branches that occur on the outer bends.

Redundant branches are removed.

This gives a naturally extended look to the form. Inner bending branches, unless they are really small, look awkward.

Continue bending the minor branches so that they conform to the emerging pad forms. This cotoneaster has very young-looking herring-bone pattern twig growth. As you wire the shape, you may want to prune some of these opposite lines to lighten each cluster so that they relate better to each other as 'aged' structures. The thinning relieves the appearance amazingly.

When all the wired zones are bent into position, you can prune the contour of each branch to achieve further unity. Take your time over this, and when you have finished make sure that the branch junctions with the trunk line are clear. Check again for any dangling twig lines and remove them.

Quite often after you have completed the finer touches you realize the main trunk line has lost position and is trying to rise. Do two things if this happens. First, slit through the bark (see under Wiring, page 14), making the cut along the trunk

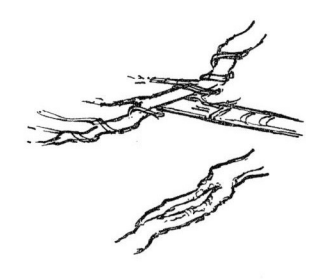

Slit the bark on the trunk so that the scar tissue holds the line.

The wired tree. The trunk has an additional guy wire to hold the angle.

on the underside. The scar tissue makes the section rigid. Second, fix a guy wire from the descending trunk line to a point near the roots. Protect both tied points with friction pads. This will correct the trunk line and hold it down.

Feed the cotoneaster with 0–10–10 and fish emulsion to nourish the plant and encourage flowers and berries, without causing coarsened growth. One of the problems in growing *Cotoneaster horizontalis* is the tendency it has to go thick, but keeping down the nitrogen in the feed helps make fine growth. You should still get some flowers this year, even with the styling.

Let the plant develop freely in the first year to get over the shock of so much pruning. If the plant looks really strong, you can also wire some of the matchstick-thick twigs as they fatten up. De-wire the cotoneaster in early autumn.

In early spring of year 2 the branches are pruned back and the schedule in Seasonal Care (see page 65) is followed, keeping the plant slowly evolving.

In year 3 the plant may be repotted into a Cascade-form container. It is helpful to relate the plant to the vertical wall of the pot. This gives a good visual reference for the position of the foliage pads and where they need thinning, extra weight, more detail, less detail, more contour and so on. You do not have to buy the major pot at this point – you just need an idea of proportions.

Follow the schedule and in about five years you will have an outstanding tree.

A lot of refinement will be needed to lose the juvenile, herring-bone twig pattern, but in the process you can add a lot of details like small changes in growth direction, and you can cut back, thin out and gradually create real branch quality.
Small or Shohin Bonsai *Cotoneaster horizontalis* makes a lovely shohin bonsai. The tiny leaves, flowers and berries work well as small-scale features, and such small plants can be planted on a rock, either singly, or in clumps and groups of trunks.

You will need: see above.
Season: early spring as buds swell.

Beginning with container-grown stock as before, set the plant on the turntable and check the trunk or trunks. You are looking for a line that has movement right at the base. It does not matter how many masking side branch lines there may be, these can all go, but in the meantime their presence will have thickened the selected trunk. The chosen line will end up 10–5cm (4–6in). All other branches and trunks are removed.

A container-grown cotoneaster.

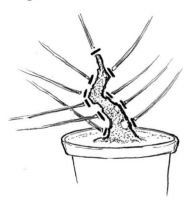

The plan is to create a Shohin bonsai with a good trunk. Remove all branches.

As you prune, look for branch lines that offer a change of trunk direction and, if it is used, a stepped taper line. You can sometimes create a tapered S-bend by this means alone. It does not matter if all the branches are removed in finding the trunk line – they will soon sprout again – but you must seal all cuts carefully.

The buds will erupt all over the trunk, but only those in the best positions are kept. All others are rubbed off. This channels the plant's energy through the chosen growth points. Let them shoot away

until they are about 15cm (6in) long, then wire them into a downswept form and shorten growth back to 5cm (2in). Trim the side buds that are then triggered, so that their terminals align and form branch contours. Then grow the plant according to the schedule in Seasonal Care for the first and second years.

Growth is encouraged at chosen points.

Left: strong new growth is trimmed and wired. **Right:** side shoots are allowed to grow strongly and are then trimmed.

Side branches and new shoots coming through soon build the profiles.

In year 2 the cotoneaster is trimmed, wired and repotted.

Repot in year 3, reducing the pot depth by half – from 23cm (9in) in diameter by 15cm (6in) deep to 23cm (9in) in diameter by 8cm (3in) deep – then follow the schedule again. It will soon be a beautiful

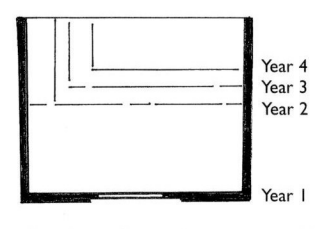

Progressively smaller sizes of container are used in years 1 to 4.

little plant. Aim for a tree that has an overall height of about 15cm (6in) and a branch width of 20–23cm (8–9in).

In year 4 repot it into a pot about 18cm (7in) in diameter by 5cm (2in) deep. Grow for a year, then repot into the final pot. Phasing the pot size down

The cotoneaster is repotted into a final pot. The plant is 15cm (6in) high and the pot measures 18 × 10 × 5cm (7 × 4 × 2in)

and allowing the time between reductions to the root mass ensures that shock is minimal.

Bonsai Re-creation

This attractive planting of *Cotoneaster microphyllus* and the rock were planned together as a unit by Bill Jordan, who also made the fibreglass and *ciment fondu* rock. The rock shape is reminiscent of seashore and

Cotoneaster microphyllus planted on fibreglass and *ciment fondu* rocks.

A close-up of the flower of *Cotoneaster microphyllus*.

cliffs, where wind and waves have scoured holes. The form of cliff-hugging plants is well done, and they are very convincing as trees shaped by onshore gales.

HEIGHT: 8–10cm (3–4in); trunk diameter: 12–18mm (½–¾in); AGE: 8–10 years. Dimensions of fibreglass rock: approximately 60 × 60cm (24 × 24in) and about 30cm (12in) deep.

Trunk and Branch Reconstruction Raised from cuttings, the plants are examples of *Cotoneaster microphyllus*, which produces these fine, deep red fruit. The variety is handled identically to rockspray cotoneaster *(C. horizontalis)*.

The form of the trunk is created by feeding and watering the cuttings heavily to make them grow fast. When growth is fat and lush the plants are severely shortened and a mass of buds erupts from the trunk. These are grown freely for a season and then the plants are pruned again.

The second pruning is more selective and the

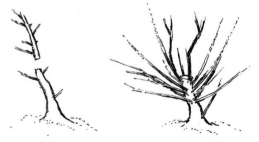

Left: the trunks are shortened in a period of strong growth. **Right:** the resulting mass of shoots is grown freely for a season.

crowded areas are thinned. The remaining branches are pruned for spread and line. The aim is to form shallow domes of foliage on top of compact, characterful trunks. Trunk lines are often pruned back hard to make radical changes in growth direction. This may be repeated after re-growth to make crooked forms. Take your time and assemble plants that work together and harmonize with the rock.

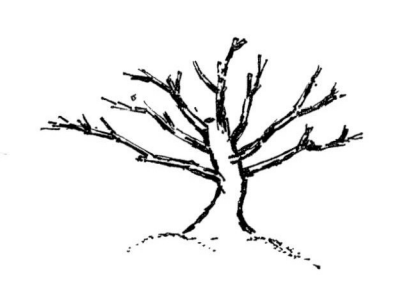

The second pruning is selective.

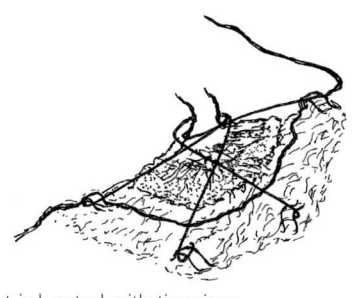

The plant is located with tie-wires.

The shoots are trimmed to make shallow, twiggy domes.

systems making sure it penetrates and covers the roots. Contour the paste, and if any plants are vertical positioned beneath overhangs, fasten screen netting with wires to support the rootball.

The trunks are often pruned hard to form crooked lines.

Plastic screen netting is used to support the rootball if there are erosion problems or steep planting angles.

Mosses and accent plants may be added to the contoured paste, with additional paste used to embed them as necessary.

The process is repeated as necessary.

Mosses and underplantings are added as the final touch.

The Planting The rock is constructed with wire location loops bedded into the fibreglass around the planned planting area. This is a great time saver. The plastic screen used for drainage holes is used to support the root mass positioned on the rock face.

Root-prune the cotoneasters lightly and check them for position on the planting zone. Smear peat and soil paste over the planting area, position each plant and tie it to the rock with wires from the location loops. Add more paste and soil to the root

Aftercare Lightly spray the plants and root zones regularly to keep humidity up until the roots can take hold. Place the rock planting in the shade, but after a month or so, give it more light.

Do not wire for a season. This allows the plant to key to the rock without movement. Display the planting in a *suiban* with fine sand or water.

The rock construction method is covered in my book *The Art of Bonsai* (Ward Lock, 1990).

Crab Apple

The crab apple *(Malus)* is an easy and rewarding tree to grow as bonsai, and although the branches tend to disappear with the spread of leaves, the two wonderful displays of flower and fruit more than compensate. To see a single spray of flowers up close is really to appreciate an orchard for the first time. At full size, the orchard is a vast, fragrant spread of pink, which simply overwhelms the senses. Seen close to, the single, scented, pink-white bunch of flowers is breath-taking.

Most of the crab apples available in the bonsai trade are from field-grown, grafted trees. They are grafted as a reliable and quick way to obtain flowering plants that are true to type. The Nagasaki crab apple *(Malus baccata,* syn. *M. cerasifera)* is commonly imported as 'Hime-Ringo', and it is usually available with a stocky trunk and a good spread of whorled, wired and pruned branches. This gives you the best start in developing a bonsai. However, there are excellent grafted plants intended for landscaping and garden use available in general nurseries. You may not find a Nagasaki crab apple, but there are many others.

The tree is easy to work with in most respects. In training the most important thing to remember is

Hall's crab apple *(Malus halliana)* in a pot by Dan Barton.

to wire new growth before it hardens up. Crab apple is so brittle that there is almost no chance of shaping old shoots with wire. It is better to prune and train the resultant new shoots.

Watering and feeding are also essential. If the tree dries out in leaf and fruit, it will develop leaf burn and probably drop the fruit. Feed generously after the fruit swells – but not before, because this leads to fruit drop. It is easy to forget this, especially if you want to pamper your tree!

Most crab apples have a naturally occurring 'year off', when they fruit lightly. This is nothing to worry about, although it can be countered to some extent by thinning the number of fruit that are borne on the tree. This will also help to conserve the tree's energy. It is, however, a difficult task to do with the dark red, cherry-like fruits hanging on the bare tree.

There is a wide choice of pots for this genus. The colours discussed for all the other trees would be suitable, as would the semi-matt qualities of glazed ware. Dull yellows and off-whites do look

The first bud colour of a Nagasaki crab apple (*Malus baccata*, syn. *M. cerasifera*) is light red.

wonderful with the red fruit. A soft-contoured pot looks best, and the depth and length can be generous for both horticultural and artistic considerations.

Try Hall's crab apple (*Malus halliana*) – the pink-red flowers, dark green leaves and silver-grey trunk make it a fabulous bonsai, even though it does not fruit.

Seasonal Care

Training Styles Informal, Leaning, Semi-cascade, Cascade, Literati, Root over Rock, Twin-trunk, Raft, Root-connected, Group.

Likely Source Readily available as imported Japanese bonsai. Local nurseries will have many varieties available.

Propagation Easily propagated by grafts, quite easily by layers, and easily by division, when grown on own roots.

Type and Description A deciduous, flowering and fruiting tree.

Habitat Japan.

Trunk Young shoots are reddish-green. The bark

Later, the buds of the Nagasaki crab apple show pink and white.

A close-up of the flowers of Hall's crab apple.

matures to silvery brown and darkens and breaks into plates with age.

Foliage Leaves are spear-shaped, about 2.5–5cm (1–2in) long, serrated and deep green.

Flowers Single flowers are borne in bunches in late spring. The red buds open pink and fade to white when fully open. Fragrant. Every three or four years remove all flowers and rest the tree. It can do with it!

Fruit Fruit is sometimes very profuse. It is about cherry size and turns deep red.

Soil Three parts composted peat, two parts akadama, three parts leaf mould and two parts sand.

Potting and Repotting Young plants are repotted annually, older plants every other year. Do this in early spring.

Water Always keep crab apple damp – it likes water.

Feeding Feed every three weeks from when leaves swell until the flowering period, using half-strength Miracle-Gro or something similar. Alternate with 0–10–10. Do not feed too much before fruit swells because this can make the fruit drop. Stop feeding in the flowering period. After the flowering period, wait until the fruit swells to fingernail size, resume alternate feeds until late summer. From late summer until mid-autumn feed every two weeks with 0–10–10. Feed once a year with Trace Element Frit.

Trimming Old branches can be pruned when repotting. New shoots are pinched when they go over 2.5cm (1in) in length – just nip the terminals. Do not prune after this in the growing period otherwise non-flowering shoots are produced.

Note: as all apples scar hugely when pruned, delay old branch removal until dormancy.

Wiring Wire new growth in early summer. Older wood is very brittle. Use aluminium wire.

Position Place the crab apple in good light, but do not let it get baked in the sun. Keep out of any heavy frost.

Pests and Diseases Mealy bug, scale and aphids can appear. Spray with a mild insecticide, such as pyrethrum. Mildew can appear in hot, humid conditions. Treat by improving the air flow and by spraying with a fungicide such as Bordeaux mixture or dimethoate. Most other conditions are controllable with the use of sprays formulated for fruit trees.

Other Species There are many wonderful crab apple species to choose from, with single and double flowers, and fruit in different sizes and colours. Among those worth a look are: Hall's crab apple *(Malus halliana)* – pink-red flowers; Siberian crab apple *(M. baccata)* – white flowers, red fruit; *M. × zumi* 'Golden Hornet' – white flowers, yellow fruit.

Material Type

Choose container-grown nursery stock when the trees are in flower. If you are really organized, check the fruit during the previous autumn. It will give you a feel for the variety and how it grows. Look for trees with stocky bases that have some lower trunk movement. Look for surface roots too. These can be very nice with this species. The shapes you are most likely to find are the Informal and Leaning.

You will need: shears, saw, jin pliers, rake, wound sealant, potting soil, large prepared containers.
Season: after flowering in spring.

Remove the tree from the pot and assess it for trunk movement and the best diameter combined with the greatest root spread. The lower 30–45cm (12–18in) of trunk line are the key to the whole design.

Shortening the trunk of a container-grown crab apple from a nursery.

Comb out the soil around the surface roots so that you can see their lines. Put the tree on the turntable and check all possible viewing angles. Look for an upper branch that will work as a continuation of the trunk line when it is sawn down. When you have found the branch, saw down the trunk, making a diagonal cut. Do not cut too close to the branch line but preserve a stump. Clean up the edge of the saw cut with a scalpel, making a bevelled cut, so that the bark can heal over easily.

Shorten all the branches that are to be kept. Make the cuts above outward-facing buds. Remove all other branches but leave stumps. Remember that all apple trees make huge scar calluses if they are pruned in active growth. If you cut the branch flush at the end of the season when the healing mechanism is shutting down, the scar heals flat. Seal all cuts.

Return to the roots and comb them out. Prune away the taproot and heavy lower roots. Thin out and comb the mass outward until it is evenly distributed with no dense areas.

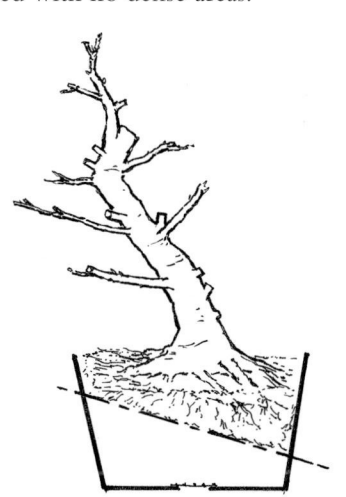

The plan is to make a Leaning bonsai. Branches that are 'keepers' are shortened and others are removed, leaving a stump for later removal. The tree is repotted and the planting is changed.

Crab apples can tolerate a lot of root reduction – up to 50 per cent of the lower roots on a healthy tree can be safely removed. If you are going to create a Leaning tree, you can induce a lot of trunk angle by making a slanting cut across the base of the root mass so that the tree sits tilted in the chosen direction.

Pot the tree up in a large temporary container, with good drainage and the suggested soil mix. The tree will need to be immobilized with tie-strings so that it does not keel over. Cushion the friction points on the trunk.

The 'Nagoya bend', with additional wiggle!

This is the moment you have been planning for, when you get to style the tree in the Leaning shape. Place the branches according to your design first. The lazy-S styling is secondary. Be careful to de-wire at the first signs of the wire biting in, which is usually four to six weeks after wiring.

After repotting, the crab apple is placed in a plastic green-house (poly-tunnel) to recover and grow freely.

Place the crab apple in a plastic greenhouse (poly-tunnel) and water it in well. The warmth and humidity in the greenhouse will make it shoot and root strongly. Make sure the tree does not sit around in static air, however, because it needs ventilation at all times. After a month or so, the tree can be moved into an airy, sunnier place. Be cautious, though: if the temperature rises, shade the tree immediately. Dappled shade is safest.

Note: check the shoot colour on the crab apple when it is shaded. If the colour appears white/green it needs light. Growth should be red-green.

Shoots are wired in early summer and are allowed to grow without trimming back. Bend branches in the downswept Nagoya style, with the branches in a lazy-S shape.

After wiring you get the first feel for the design.

Follow the water and feeding schedule outlined under Seasonal Care (see page 73) after the tree has left the greenhouse.

In year 2 shorten the upper parts of the tree. As it grows so vigorously, the tree will soon become very top-heavy if it is not pruned.

In year 2 the upper branches are shortened.

Wire new growth in early summer, using the same downswept, curving lines. Let the growth develop freely and de-wire as the wire tightens and before it bites. Continue the watering and feeding schedules.

In year 3 repot the tree. Wash the roots and check for and remove any heavy, circling lower roots. Even and prune the root mass. Prune the upper branches short and the lower branches by reducing their length by half.

The plant is then allowed free growth.

Left: wire in early summer. Right: in year 3 the upper branches are pruned short and the lower branches are halved. The tree is then repotted.

Pot up in a shallower box or temporary bonsai pot, and grow the tree according to the Seasonal Care schedule. Adjust your design with wiring or pruning as necessary. You can choose the final pot now, even if you do not get to use it for a year or two. Potters often take a long time to produce *the* perfect pot.

The final pot.

Bonsai Re-creation

HEIGHT: 60cm (24in); trunk diameter: 8cm (3in), AGE: about 20 years; flowers: white.

Trunk The Nagasaki crab apple shown overleaf is a good example of the growth structure of field-grown imported trees. The bark is smooth and free of the obvious scarring that is associated with the 'grow and chop' trunk development process.

Trunk Reconstruction Start with a three-year-old graft. This will give you a good thickness of trunk and the chance to find one with a bit of curvature. Trim the trunk short. Let the tree grow freely, then pick a well-placed branch as a leader and prune the branches. Trim the leader.

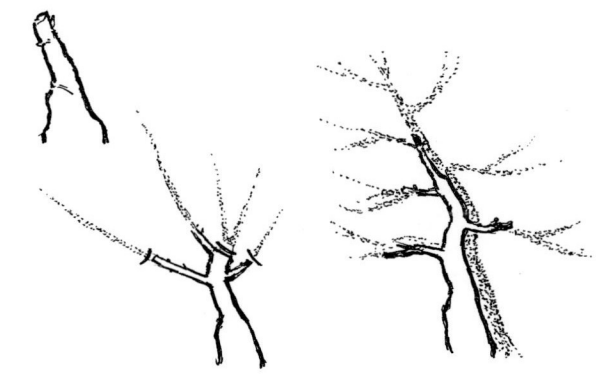

Top left: the three-year-old graft is cut short in spring. Centre: after a season, the branches and new trunk line are shortened. Right: the branches are shortened in summer and re-grown. The tree fattens as it grows taller each year.

A Nagaski crab apple *(Malus baccata, syn. M. cerasifera)* has white, lightly scented flowers.

In year 5 root-prune the tree and plant it out to grow freely. Shorten the branches in summer and let the shoots develop again.

In year 6 prune the roots again and shorten the branches. Shorten the branches in summer and wire them. De-wire in autumn.

Repeat system until the trunk is thick enough to suit the design. Build the branches slowly.

Left: side branches are added to the main branches.
Right: build the branches slowly.

A close-up of the fruit after light rain.

Branch Reconstruction The owner has retained the branches so that they are no longer in the whorled, lazy-S configuration, which is fine in setting up the form. Their training is now much more diverse and natural. In general terms, as the tree settles into a mature shape, an upturning line is more pleasing than the flatter line, which can look mechanical. There is an agreeable softness here that is quite in keeping with the line of the trunk, although the downswept line could work equally well. The grower has featured both descending and uptilted branches in a very believable impression of a tree with a vigorous crown and older, weeping lower lines.

The form of the branches is based on the lazy-S shape. This is established by wiring, pruning and

regrowing selected branches. The root system is probably a little under-developed and the owner has added rocks to the soil surface for texture and form. The pot is a good-quality Japanese unglazed yellow oval pot.

Left: branches are wired in summer and shortened.
Right: new shoots are also wired and the branch planes are quickly developed.

The dark red fruits are near to scale on the tree.

Firethorn

Like cotoneaster, pyracantha is seen everywhere in gardens and as hedging. It is a really beautiful plant seen close to, when a more limited fruit display is spread over the frame of a bonsai. In Britain you see the aptly named, amazingly orange-berried *Pyracantha* 'Orange Glow' and the vermilion-berried *P. coccinea* 'Lalandei' planted in gardens everywhere. Everyone loves them, but transfer that beauty to micro-size and you enhance and distil it into something more.

It is an easy plant to grow if you remember that the wood is brittle and new growth must be wired early. Because of the straight growth habit of the plant, it is reluctant to bend, and firethorn bonsai can be a little stiff in appearance for this reason. If the grower is prepared to cut deeply into the wood to re-grow the straighter lines, it is easy to wire them to curve them.

It is a good idea to first build the branches by pinching constantly than to worry about flower and fruit at an early stage.

There are a lot of the oriental *Pyracantha angustifolia* in the bonsai trade. As with the imported crab apples, they give the grower a head start. However,

Firethorn flowers.

Close-up of the fruit.

ordinary nurseries have good stocks of most varieties. Choose a plant with a fat trunk and simply cut it back and develop the re-growth and you will soon have a great tree.

These plants need good watering and feeding, otherwise they dry up and become miserable. Keep them damp and well fed and they grow like crazy. They can be trimmed into most styles of bonsai and work well at most sizes.

Container colour should be chosen with the brilliance of the berries in mind. The dark green leaves enhance the bright fruit and throw their colour forwards. A midnight blue glaze looks sumptuous with orange or red, and yellow is also very successful. Semi-matt glazes look better on the whole, but with a small tree, a shinier glaze can work well. Unglazed ware is also pleasing with older trees. Pyracanthas prefer deep soil, so deepish containers are best, although avoid shapes that are too geometric.

Seasonal Care

Training Styles Informal, Leaning, Semi-cascade, Cascade, Literati, Driftwood, Root over Rock, Tree on Rock, Twin-trunk, Raft, Root-connected, Group.

Likely Sources Pyracanthas are readily available as garden plants, as imported Japanese bonsai and as local nursery stock.

Propagation It is easy to propagate from cuttings and by layering or division.

Type and Description An evergreen shrub, which can reach almost small tree size. It can be deciduous in cold areas.

Habitat Different species and varieties are native to China, Asia, America, Britain and France.

Trunk Young shoots are green and the bark ages to grey and becomes thick. Branches are brittle.

Foliage The leaves vary from narrow, to spear-shaped to narrowly obovate according to species. They are all dark green and shiny. Some older foliage is shed each year.

Flowers Flowers are white, small and borne in sprays.

Fruit The berries are yellow to red according to variety. They are holly berry size and they hang in bunches often into winter.

Soil Two parts sand, three parts leaf mould, three parts composted peat and two parts compost or akadama gives a rich and well-drained soil.

Potting and Repotting When potting and repotting use medium deep or deeper containers. This plant likes cool roots. Root-prune young plants annually, and older plants every other year in early to mid-spring.

Water Keep damp at all times. Pyracanthas like water, so spray the foliage too.

Feeding When leaves swell feed every two weeks until the flowering period with Miracle-Gro or a similar feed. Alternate with 0–10–10. After the flowers fade and the berries swell, let them make half size then recommence alternate feeds until late summer. From late summer until mid-autumn, feed every two weeks with 0–10–10. Feed once every year with Trace Element Frit.

Trimming Old branches can be pruned when repotting. Trim the soft growth back to the branch contour. This type of pruning is done in spring – late spring is the best time.

Note: remove volunteer inner buds if they are not required to improve the shape.

Wiring Wire new growth in early to midsummer, bearing in mind that older wood is very brittle. Use aluminium wire.

Position Place pyracanthas in good light, but do not let the plants get baked. Rotate the trees when they are in fruit to get even fruit colour. Keep out of heavy frost.

Pests and Diseases Aphids and scale insect can be a problem. Use a mild insecticide such as pyrethrum.

Species There are many forms suitable for bonsai. Among the most popular are: *Pyracantha angustifolia* – orange-yellow berries; *P. atalantioides* – scarlet berries; *P. coccinea* 'Lalandei' – orange-red berries; *P.*

'Orange Glow' – bright orange berries; *P. rogersiana* 'Flava' – bright yellow berries.

Material Type

There are several ways of starting with a firethorn: you can take thick cuttings or layers from a garden plant; you can buy one from Japan; or you can develop it from cut-down nursery stock. We have already created bonsai in that way twice, so let us begin with a thick branch cutting.

It helps when you are looking at material if you have some shape in mind. Occasionally, if you are lucky, the material itself can suggest a way of going, and Shohin or Root over Rock are possibilities.

The aim is to grow the firethorn as a Shohin bonsai in the Root over Rock style. The heavy cutting shows a root callus.

You are looking for short, characterful branch terminals, such as those that can be found on wall shrubs that have been cut back regularly. If you cannot locate a neighbourhood source, you may be reduced to buying a plant to use as a stock plant. If you have to pay, you may as well get a bonsai in the first place.

The tools and equipment you will need and the method are described under How Bonsai are Created (see page 17).

Starting with year 2, after the cuttings are well established as separately potted plants, you can begin their styling. It is rather fun to aim for short and spreading plants that look good as Shohin or Root over Rock or both.

In this case you almost certainly are going to find a lot of basal shoots and a mass of criss-cross branching. Reduce the trunk to a skeleton by pruning so that you can find the shortest tapered line. Seal all cuts and then develop the tree as suggested for the Shohin cotoneaster (see page 68), but instead of repotting, leave the tree untouched until the top is developed enough. This encourages roots that are long enough to set comfortably astride the rock.

The cutting is allowed to grow freely.

As the tree develops, leave it in the pot to form long roots.

In, say, spring of year 4, when the tree is ready, what should you do? First, select a rock. There are wonderful pictures of small bonsai over rock in collections of photographs from Japanese exhibitions. The combination of shapes is the primary thing. Firethorns are textured plants, and busy stones are visually irritating with them. It is best to find smoothly contoured and textured stones. But where do you find such a rock? The answer can be right under your nose. One of the beauties of small bonsai is that everything is scaled down, so instead of a huge rock, you are looking for something about the size of a doughnut – and that is a bit easier to find.

Stone merchants and landscape gardeners often have suitable rock material, there are quarries to check, and the stones in your back garden are probably usable. Just look. Stones must be clean and free of contaminants like sea salt. The colour should be quiet. The ideal stone should stand well, possess a saddle-like depression in which the tree will sit, and have some natural folds and fissures along which the roots can be carried.

The rock has a good shape and a suitable planting 'saddle'.

Next, check the rock and plant together. The tree may hug the rock, blending with the lines, or it be a more overpowering presence with the rock as the minor element. Either way, this avoids the dullness of two equally dominant features.

Take the firethorn out of the pot. Rake out and roughly prune the root mass to fit the rock. Try the tree in the 'saddle' and in various spots on the stone, draping the roots in bunches down the fissures so that they will enter the soil naturally.

Try the tree in different positions...

Left: better... **Right:** good.

When you are happy, make a note of the position; if possible, take a Polaroid photograph. Remove the plant and keep it damp. Prepare some peat and soil mixed to a paste with water; adding a small amount of clay to the mixture can be helpful.

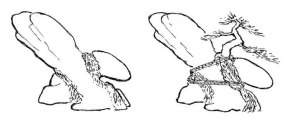

Left: spread paste along the planting fissures. **Right:** the plant is secured in its position with string.

Wrap aluminium foil around the roots and press it down.

Smear the selected rock fissures with the paste and position the tree, tying it in position with soft string. Divide the roots into bunches and conduct them down along the fissures and tuck the tips under the rock. Smear more paste over the root-filled fissures and wrap aluminium foil around them.

Half-fill the container with the suggested soil mix (see page 15) and place the rock–tree unit on the bed of soil. Steady the tree as you plant it so that the roots stay in position. Press the aluminium foil wrapping down around the roots so that the roots are slightly squashed. This will make them spread sideways and grip the rock. If you do not do this, the roots will stand rigid and away from the rock face.

Place the rock–tree unit in a deep planting box.

Add more soil all around the foil wrapped rock–tree unit and top up, making sure the foil is open at the top for watering. Firm the soil gently to settle it evenly against the foil, so that it presses onto the roots.

Place the tree in a plastic greenhouse and water it in well. Keep it in dappled shade with good air circulation, and do not be in too much of a hurry to water the soil again until you see some dryness. After a month, follow Seasonal Care (see pages 81–2).

In year 2 check the roots over the rock, beginning by removing the top plank of the box. Remove the soil to the same depth and peel away the foil, also to the same depth. You should see roots beginning to spread and become established. Look for roots that are fattening and joining up. Leave the rest of the roots covered. Roots fatten if they are wet. Put a pad of sphagnum moss over the exposed tree base and root area. Continue with the seasonal care schedules.

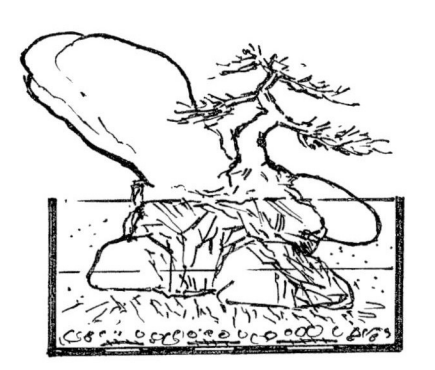

In year 2 remove the top plank, the exposed soil and the foil.

In year 3 remove another plank strip from the box, remove the soil and peel away the foil to the same level. Check the roots again. You should see some appreciable widening of the roots in the fissures. Leave for another season before removing the last of the foil and checking your handiwork. The original soft string will have rotted away by now, and there should be a good formation of maturing roots clutching the stone.

In year 4 the rock–tree unit is repotted, leaving a square pad of root below the rock.

The final pot.

There is going to be a lot of root to contend with beneath the rock and the best course is to repot, but keep the root mass on the large side for this final year. Do not break up the pad of root beneath the stone because the rock–tree unit needs a square base to stand on. You can thin it out the next time.

Bonsai Re-creation

The firethorn tree overleaf was started by John Castle in Alameda, California. He took the tree to a workshop with Dan Robinson for the first styling. I saw the tree in 1983 and brought it to Britain.
HEIGHT: 84cm (33in); trunk diameter: 25cm (10in); AGE: about 20 years.

Trunk The trunk has a lot of character, with thick bark and a hollowed area of natural damage on the lower trunk. The foot of the trunk features an old root section that swells to a massive 30cm (12in) spread.

TRUNK RECONSTRUCTION The trunk was generated from a 6m (20ft) garden plant that was cut down to 76cm (30in). The diameter at the soil level was 30cm (12in). The trunk was transplanted into a temporary container and carefully looked after to speed recovery. After a season, when it was well rooted and firm in the container, the trunk was tapered and hollowed with an electric chain saw. The carving was refined a little with a router.

Left: the plant is cut down to 76cm (30in) and transplanted.
Right: plant the firethorn in a box and allow it to become established.

After restyling, the trunk has more power.

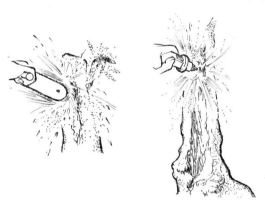

Left: after a year the trunk is carved for taper and to continue the natural hollowing. **Right:** the carved area is refined with a router.

The tree was shaded after carving and was fed and watered well and allowed another season of free growth. In the following year, it was wired and transplanted into a large bonsai pot and the basic shape was almost complete.

Left: the firethorn was allowed another growth period to recover from styling. **Right:** after wiring, the tree was repotted into a large bonsai pot.

The firethorn as seen from the back.

of bold profiles that balance the heavy trunk.

A heavy trunk like this can be grown by using the fast trunk development method. You can start with material from any of the four sources discussed earlier. I grew a pine with an 8cm (3in) diameter trunk in five years, using a huge box inside a plastic greenhouse, and this is slow compared to firethorns.

The proportions are completely different after the height of the firethorn was reduced.

After it was imported, the branch planes were further developed by trimming and by wiring new growth. I transplanted it into the Japanese Kataoka pot in 1984 and carried on refining the basic form.

It was during a class in 1993 that I got the idea of reducing the height of the tree, which was, as it turned out, a good decision. My students were quite staggered to see a well-proportioned trunk section cut down, but, as I pointed out, the apex was weak and made the whole design a little too tall. The cut dramatically changed the tree and emphasized the powerful lower trunk. I left the stump of the former trunk line to carve a flowing shape with some spiralling that harmonized with the trunk movement.

Branch development is largely a matter of selecting and growing on from the buds that constantly pop out on the trunk. Although it is essentially the now familiar lazy-S formation, the branch planes are being encouraged to become very dense by continual pinching back. The branches work best as a series

White and Red Hawthorn

The white flowers of hawthorn are a familiar sight in the spring landscape, and through bonsai you can bring this home with you and enjoy it. Old hawthorns are fairly easily collected where animals have done a fair job of rough shaping. Pastures and wilder countryside are good hunting places.

The white flowers of the wild common hawthorn *(Crataegus monogyna)* often display a pink tinge. They offer a subtle colour, which is worth searching for. If the trees are well fed, the red berries will hang on into winter. The bark on old trees is rough, and if they have been grazed over, the branches will be densely twigged. Watch out for prickly thorns!

Red hawthorn, *Crataegus laevigata* 'Paul's Scarlet', is best obtained from the bonsai trade or as young grafted whips from general nurseries. Alternatively, you can graft it yourself. It is a vigorous, double-flowered form, with bright red flowers.

Both white and red forms are tremendous as bonsai. The collected, single-flowered white has an elegance and a wild charm that the domestic, double red cannot equal, but if you grow a red hawthorn in the ground for a few years it soon

A close-up of the white flowers with pink variation.

develops a great trunk. As a bigger tree, the double red flowers are not so overpowering and the bark roughens at last with age.

The wood is very brittle, and this means that old trees very often need deep pruning to change growth direction. However, they bud back profusely and the strong re-growth is easily styled and quickly matures.

Hawthorns love food and water. This means you can fatten it quickly. However the wood fattens fast when it is fed with nitrogen, and taper and scale soon vanish. For example, if you are extending the branches of an old collected tree, do not overfeed it or the character of the fine old branches will be lost. Use low nitrogen feeds.

Make sure that the soil drains well. Use a rich soil, but one that breathes, otherwise the tree will be badly effected.

I have a fondness for yellow or off-white glazes with this species, although a lot depends on the quality of the colour. If it is subtle, with good variations of shading, a dull or deep blue or celadon green can work. The form of the pot can be quite strong to balance the enormous visual energy of the collected trunks.

Seasonal Care

Training Styles Informal, Leaning, Wind-swept, Semi-cascade, Cascade, Literati, Driftwood, Root over Rock, Twin-trunk, Raft, Root-connected, Group.

Likely Source Hawthorns are readily available as natural, local nursery stock, as own grafts or as imported Japanese bonsai.

Propagation The red hawthorn is easy to top graft onto seedling *Crataegus oxyacantha* stock. The white form is easily propagated by layering and division.

Type and Description A small, deciduous, flowering and fruiting tree.

Habitat Asia Minor and Europe.

Trunk The young growth is green, becoming

Red hawthorn flowers.

A close-up of the flower buds of white hawthorn.

silvery-buff. Older bark is orangey-brown, and it can become quite fissured and heavy.

Foliage Young shoots are reddish and the leaves have four lobes on each side and are deeply divided. Mature leaves are deep green. Thorns are up to 2.5cm (1in) long.

Flowers The fragrant flowers appear in late spring. Buds are borne in dense bunches, and individual florets open wide with dark anthers. Collected plants often show some pink flowers.

Fruit The fruits are dark red and about the size of holly berries.

Species There are several hundred species in America and nearly a hundred more through Asia and Europe. Among the best for bonsai are: *Crataegus laevigata* 'Paul's Scarlet' – double scarlet flowers; *C. l.* 'Rosea' – pink single flowers; *C. phaenopyrum* 'Washington Thorn' – white flowers, red fruit.

Soil Two parts sand, three parts leaf mould, three parts composted peat and two parts compost or akadama gives a light but rich soil.

Note: if the soil feels spongy when gripped in the fist, the texture is right. If it compresses without crumbling, add more sand and composted peat.

Potting and Repotting Repot each year in early spring.

Water Hawthorns like plenty of water.

Feeding Feed every two weeks from when leaves first swell until the flowering period with half-strength Miracle-Gro or a similar feed. Alternate with 0–10–10. After the flowers fade and the berries swell recommence alternate feeds until late summer. From late summer until mid-autumn feed every two weeks with 0–10–10. Feed once every year with Trace Element Frit.

Trimming Old branches can be pruned when repotting. Trim new growth back to the branch contour as early as your design permits. In maintenance pruning, new growth is reduced to two leaves.

Hawthorn makes huge healing scars, so if you need to restyle it in growth, use my two-stage system (see under trimming holly, page 99). Do not prune too much after late spring, because this makes the plant form non-flowering shoots.

Wiring Wire new growth in early to midsummer. Remember that older wood is very brittle. Use aluminium wire.

Position Place hawthorns in good light, but do not let it get too hot. Keep out of heavy frost.

Pests and Diseases Aphids and scale insects can be a problem. Spray with an insecticide such as pyrethrum. Peach leaf curl can be treated with lime sulphur as a pre-emergent spray; Bordeaux mixture also works.

Material Type

Some of the most exciting hawthorn material can be found in the wild. The quality of the natural trees is outstanding, and all sizes can be found. Some examples have gained a great reputation for flowering bonsai. Most of the examples are large, but there are superb trees in the Shohin to medium sizes, with 30cm (12in) trunks, to be found.

The key to shaping such wild material is to relate the branches to the trunk without having recourse to rigid styling. This is a challenge, the greatest part of which is not to smother the natural feeling of the plant.

The collecting method was described in Part I (see pages 33–5), so let us take a look at developing a tree collected around 1970. This is not a really 'wild' shape, which is discussed under the re-creation on page 96, but it is an example of the smaller size. It is also a Twin-trunk. I have seen wonderful, sheep-chewed hawthorns that any grower of Shohin would pay the earth for – but why are they always growing in protected areas?

In 1970, I was on a desolate hillside in Wales, which was covered in sheep and hawthorn. The

The white hawthorn, aged about 40 years, 50cm (20in) high and with a trunk diameter of 10cm (4in) photographed in 1993.

ground was a little marshy but seemed stable enough. The tree was located by a feeder stream that more or less followed a bed to the main river in the valley below. It was one of a group of three individual trunks, all much dwarfed. This was an occasion when instead of the full tool kit, I had only a Swiss Army pocket knife and a plastic bag ready for the roots. The plant was easy to collect and came up with a good ball of moss-covered root fibre. There was no taproot as such, but there were several heavy laterals that were no match for the little saw blade in the knife.

Digging like this is not the easiest way to collect, but it can work with a small plant, if you take time to cut around and under the trunk. The temptation is always to just grasp the trunk and lean backwards, and perhaps not surprisingly, there are quite a lot of people who do it that way! The rest of us less skilled growers are better off if we retain some roots.

The roots were certainly wet enough. As I crouched by the tree I was troubled by the fact the horizon seemed tilted at 30 degrees. I found I was standing on a raft of grass and tree roots that was gradually sinking under my weight. I covered the distance to the higher ground in rather better than Olympic speed, to the great enjoyment of the sheep.

Back at the nursery, in a plastic greenhouse, I carefully inspected the hawthorn for transplant damage. Amazingly there was very little. The root nucleus under the forked trunk base was compact and fibrous, and there were the woody laterals, which were carefully recut to clean away the ragged saw marks.

The trunks stood 23cm (9in) and 10cm (4in) from the trunk base. Even the apices were rounded off and covered in bark! The roots and the top of the tree were in perfect balance. The twin trunks were as compact as the roots: sheep and deer had chewed the branches back to nothing. There were a few branch spurs, about 5cm (2in) long, with woody 'lollipops' on the end of each. Each swollen terminal was covered in sprouting buds, as, on closer inspection, was the trunk. So there was no need to reduce any branches to balance the root loss.

The roots were soaked overnight in a bucket of Superthrive vitamin B1 transplant solution. I used a

The original root mass of a collected hawthorn, with laterals and compact, fibrous area.

plastic seed tray, 36 × 23cm (14 × 9in), for the first container and passed tie-wires up through the drainage holes in the tray.

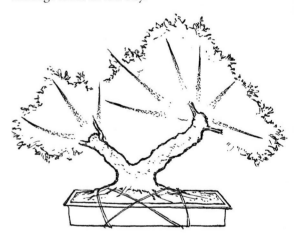

The tree was allowed to grow freely.

The hawthorn was lifted carefully out of the bucket containing the transplant solution and drained to remove the excess water. It was planted using the suggested soil mix with some extra sand added. The tie-wires were criss-crossed over the root mass, passing over friction pads to protect the rough bark and hold the plant very well. The hawthorn was top misted but not watered for a couple of days to give the roots a chance to become established.

The tree was placed under a growing bench in the plastic greenhouse (poly-tunnel) and kept shaded and well ventilated. The humidity helped the tree settle, and the buds pushed and the shoots took off like rockets. After a couple of weeks it was moved into better light, and after a month it was grown on a bench in the greenhouse in dappled shade. The new growth was cut back in autumn.

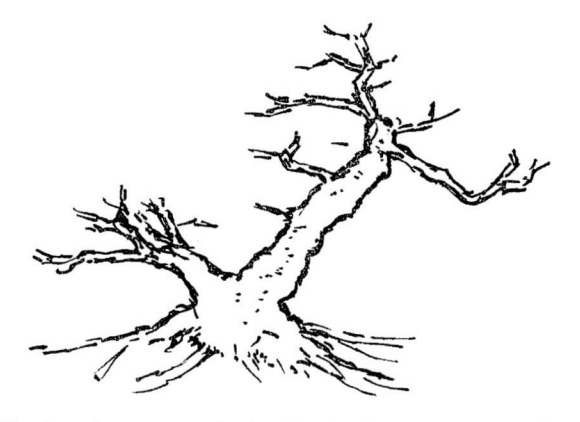

The branches were cut back without wiring every year until roots formed.

In year 2 feeding began a month after leaf growth. There is always the chance that the tree may be living on stored energy and will fail to grow in the second year. Not so with this one. It turned into a hedge and I used to take shears to it to keep some semblance of control.

In the summer of the second year, the tie-wires were un-twisted and the trunk was gently rocked to check the root growth from the degree of resistance. There was no resistance, despite all that top growth, so training was confined to pruning back to outward-facing buds and the tie-wires were put back, the tree was fed and watered.

This process continued for seven years. Then in the seventh summer, there was a carpet of fine roots filling the container. Why? The answer is the plant was a lot older than I had at first imagined and took its own sweet time.

There had been time to visualize the shape I wanted, and this season saw the new shoots wired for the first time. What a difference it made. The simple grow-and-cut system I had been forced to follow had created stocky, short branches and the wired lines looked good with them. I did no pruning during that year but de-wired the branches as needed and just trimmed the terminals back in autumn.

The growth was repeatedly cut so that the lower bud grew and curved up.

Next year I had one cluster of flowers and it was wonderful. The side buds developed into branches and were wired and trimmed and in a year I suddenly had a tree. I followed the Seasonal Care schedule for a year and repotted the tree for the first time, nine years after collection! So if at first...

After seven years! The shape is really there now, but the permanent branch frame still needs work.

The tree needs a denser 'winter-viewing' silhouette and a shorter, deeper pot.

The red hawthorn in the spring of 1997.

Bonsai Re-creation

Height: 64cm (25in); trunk diameter 8cm (3in); AGE: quoted as 40 years but probably 15 years.

Trunk Reconstruction The trunk of the red hawthorn *(Crataegus laevigata* 'Paul's Scarlet') was originally a cut-down graft. I imported it as a specimen bonsai in 1982 and would guess that it had been about 4.6m (15ft) high when it was cut down for bonsai styling. The trunk angle had been planted to lean sharply back from the base to the cut. The re-grown trunk line had been trained to come forward before being shaped into an upward, compact S. There was an approach-grafted second trunk.

Branch Reconstruction The branches had all been grown from buds popping out from the short-ened trunk. They were trained in soft curves that

The left elevation shows the twin trunk developed from a low graft. It features a rounded head of complementary branches.

The side view shows the abrupt change of angle, the extent of the present carving and the grafted second trunk.

I grew some branches on, pruned others short and thinned out some of the whorled lines. The stumps were allowed to dry out naturally and were entirely removed in autumn, avoiding the heavy callus tissue that is formed after close pruning in active growth. This enhanced the aged feel of the tree. Diversity is the natural pattern of old trees.

The stump on the shortened trunk bothered me. I lived with it for a time but eventually a hopeful prod with a finger nail discovered soft rotted tissue! It was time to get out the router! On close inspection, the stump really was a beast. It had been rounded in an attempt to make it blend with the re-grown upper trunk line, but all this did was to draw attention to the knobbly appearance.

Carving was very easy. I began by removing the flap of wound compound that had kept the wood wet and caused the rot, and after that, carving was almost too easy – the wood crumbled away. The aim

sity of branch form linked by a common theme.

The secondary trunk was trained and was then grafted very low down to balance the form of the main trunk.

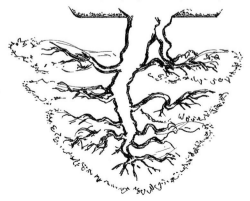

matched the trunk, but there were too many whorled lines. Together, they had been so well styled that the effect had become mechanical, which is a common fault in bonsai styling. The trick is to create a diver-

The original stump was now rotted.

The tree after a year or two. The tree looks older because further directional pruning has added the random branch detailing seen in old hawthorns. The branch lines have been selectively extended to balance the design. The twin-trunk looks better as a back detail.

I carved with the grain, contouring the wood to lose the knobby look. The carved area works far better with the shape and texture of the trunk.

was to open the area with lines of fine carving that followed the grain direction, losing that knob forever. This was carried out in a single carving session and the effect was much better.

After the trunk carving session was completed, the tree was repotted into an excellent pot by Merv Brown. The muted grey-yellow glaze suited the colours in the hollowed trunk. A new trunk aspect was chosen, which allowed the softer line to show. The hawthorn now feels like an old collected apricot and has finally lost the 'newly made' look.

The white hawthorn in 1986.

Bonsai Re-creation

HEIGHT: 60cm (24in): trunk diameter 10cm (4in): AGE: about 40 years.

The white hawthorn shown above and opposite was collected and styled by Bill Jordan. The first photograph shows the tree immediately after it was established and first styled in 1986. The second picture shows the tree after 10 years. The forms of trunk and branches have been well resolved, and they work with an entirely typical display of hawthorn characteristics. One of the reasons the tree is so successful is that Bill has fitted the branches and strong trunk together as a unit, rather than forcing the tree into a particular style. Another reason is that he has kept the elusive wild feeling of the tree.

The pot, by Gordon Duffett, blends beautifully in colour and feeling with the old tree. Both these hawthorns show the importance of the union between the right pot and the refined tree, where the pot, although interesting in itself, does not dominate.

The same tree in 1996.

Deciduous Holly

The deciduous Japanese holly *(Ilex serrata)* is not as well known as it deserves. It is a lovely plant and, when grown as a bonsai, conveys a tree image very successfully. It can be encouraged to produce a heavy trunk or it can, with equal success, be allowed to remain slender and elegant, and structured branches with many fine twigs are easily developed. The bark becomes silver-grey, and as the leaves fall the bright red berries borne on the bare twigs are very attractive.

There are some snags. It is a bit brittle and rather delicate to handle when wiring, and because the trees are different sexes it is necessary to keep the female adjacent to a male tree during the flowering period. In most parts of Britain, providing a pollinator is not usually a problem, but if you want true pollination, plant a handful of berries from a female deciduous holly and this will soon give you predominantly male seedlings. You can, of course, obtain a male deciduous holly from a good tree nursery.

Dull blue or yellow containers set off the berries. Always choose containers with soft lines that complement the mood of the tree.

A close-up of the fruit.

Seasonal Care

Training Styles Informal, Leaning, Wind-swept, Root over Rock, Twin-trunk, Raft, Root-connected, Group.

Likely Source Deciduous holly is readily available as imported Japanese bonsai; a specialist nursery may have stock.

Propagation It is easy to propagate from cuttings and from seed or by layering or division.

Type and Description A small, deciduous, flowering and fruiting tree.

Habitat Japan.

Trunk Young shoots are flushed with dark red, maturing to smooth, light grey bark.

Foliage The oval leaves have wavy edges – there are no prickles. The leaves are yellow-green and become splashed with dark purple-red towards autumn. There is often some colour before leaf-fall. The tree becomes finely twigged.

Flowers Flowers are small, white and borne singly or in clusters. They tend to be insignificant.

Fruit Fruit is bright red and typically holly sized. It can be very prolifically produced, and the tree looks wonderful in fruit after the leaves have fallen.

Cultivars Japanese winterberry (*Ilex serrata* f. *leucocarpa*) has white berries. Dwarf forms are available through the bonsai trade.

Soil Three parts sand, five parts mixed composted peat and leaf mould and two parts akadama will provide the richness the tree needs, but as always, screen out the lumps to give a spongy texture. It is permissible to adjust the mix with more peat or sand until it stays open when gripped in the fist.

Potting and Repotting Repot young trees every year and older trees every other year. Early to mid-spring is the best period.

Water Keep this tree damp. Spray the leaves in dry weather.

Feeding Hollies need steady feeding. The female trees bear the berries, and if there are to be flowers and fruit, there must be a male pollinator. This means hunting around a bit. However, because in Britain at least, there are many holly trees in gardens, pollinating usually is provided naturally.

Feed when leaves swell until the tiny white flowers appear, using half-strength Miracle-Gro, 0–10–10 and fish emulsion, alternately every 10 days. Wait until the berries are formed, then feed with normal strength 0–10–10 and half-strength fish emulsion alternately every 10 days until mid-autumn.

Trimming Hollies produce numerous new inner buds. Check the position of these and keep any that will help the design, but remove all the others. The reason for this and the low nitrogen feeding routine is because hollies fatten fast and fine twigs and taper can easily be lost. By thinning out, the tree has less work to do and does not 'muscle-up'.

New shoots are trimmed back to two leaves or so early in the season. Older branches are removed at repotting time or they are removed when they are in active growth using a two-step system. Hollies grow fast and therefore produce huge callus tissue when cut back. The method I use to get round this is, first, to shorten the redundant branch, keeping a stump 5cm (2in) long, which is left unsealed to dry out. Second, I trim the branch flush with the trunk at the end of the active growing period. The plant has less energy at this time and the healing bark tissue produced is thin.

Wiring Wire new growth in June. Older wood is very brittle. Use aluminium wire.

Position Place holly in good light, but do not let it get burned by the sun. Keep out of frost.

Pests and Diseases Essentially trouble-free, although scale insects or aphids are sometimes problems. Use an insecticide such as pyrethrum.

Other Species There is a beautiful deciduous species, *Ilex verticillata*, known as winterberry or black alder, which looks spectacular when the fruit remains after leaf-fall. Most of the evergreen holly species are worth trying, too.

Material Type

An interesting approach is to buy an imported tree and use it in a dual role, as a bonsai and as a stock plant for cuttings. The trick is to keep one cutting from the initial batch to use as a stock plant so that you do not to spoil your tree by repeatedly taking cuttings.

Deciduous holly is easily raised from cuttings, so follow the general method described under Propagation (see pages 20–9). However, let us ring the changes and start with a thick holly cutting and develop a very specific Literati.

The image of a tree I failed to order from Japan has always stayed with me. It was about 60cm (2ft) high, with two trunks and an overall diameter at the base of 8cm (3in). The features that made it magical for me were the proportion of the two trunks and the shape of the taller one. I thought it would be interesting to try to a reconstruction: a Twin-trunk Literati.

An over-developed, imported deciduous holly bonsai, which could lose a few branches. The plan is to re-create a Twin-trunk Literati remembered from 1968.

Deciduous holly trees usually produce a lot of basal suckers and lower branches, and these can be readily rooted as cuttings with large bases. The technique is to remove a branch or sucker so that it still has a 'shield' of live bark tissue attached – what gardeners call a 'heel'. I suspect that the tree I liked had been started this way.

The tools and equipment you will need are described under *How Bonsai are Created* (see pages 16–17).
Season: early spring.

Select some redundant branches and slice them off the tree, scooping out some live bark behind the cut. Look for branches with side shoots – there are usually a lot with this species – but if you do not find any, they can always be produced later by beheading a well-rooted cutting.

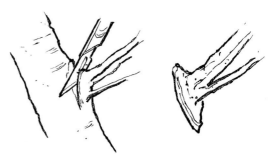

Left: scooping out a lower branch. **Right:** the scooped-out branch with its intact bark.

These heavier cuttings are given more insertion depth than lighter ones, but they are otherwise prepared and treated in the standard manner. They can be 13–15cm (5–6in) long. Trim back existing side shoots.

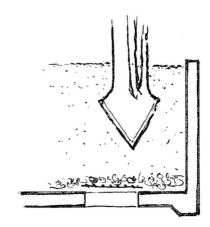

The branch is inserted as a heavy cutting with lots of space. The base is wedge cut, but the original basal flare is retained.

Hollies throw a heavy root callus and generally root after a month or so. After the plants have generated strong lateral roots, transplant them into individual pots, using the suggested soil mixture (see page 15).

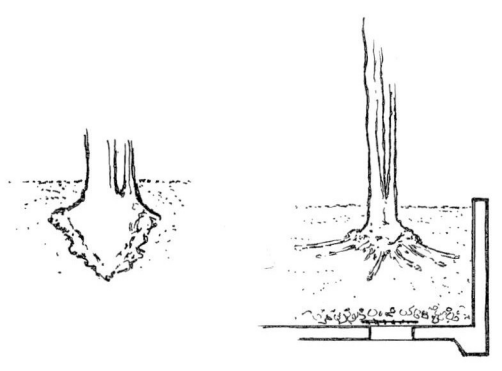

Left; A heavy root callus forms. **Right;** The primary roots spread out rapidly.

Our reconstruction starts with examining each cutting to find the plant. The original had quite widely separated trunk lines. The minor trunk was short and had a rounded head of foliage. The main trunk line was four times the height and bare of branches except for the top, which terminated with another rounded head. The minor trunk was actually a simple clump, with a number of upturned branches forming the low crown. The major trunk was a single, rising line that twisted and turned. It had a blend of curved and straighter areas.

Left: the young cutting/tree is transplanted. **Right:** each tree is assessed.

The first step is to shorten the lesser trunk line quite sharply, reducing it by about half. Prune above an outward-facing bud and leave a stump. Holly is one of the trees that makes a big scar callus. Look

under Seasonal Care for suggestions on handling this problem (see page 99). The taller trunk is pruned less, by taking about 2.5cm (1in) from the terminal.

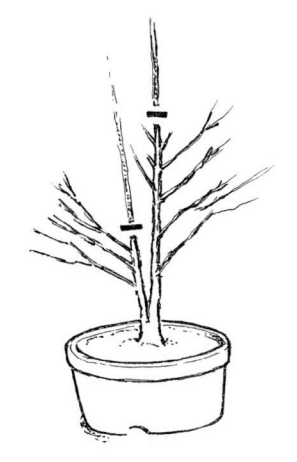

The trunks are shortened.

Place the holly in a plastic greenhouse (poly-tunnel), where the forcing effect will help the development of a lot of buds. Feed the plant and let it grow freely. When the new shoots are about 10cm (4in) long, the plant can have the first proper grooming. This is a thinning-out exercise, done with fine scissors, followed by basic wiring.

Left: the tree is encouraged to fill out. **Right:** the branch/twig structure is thinned.

Put the holly on a turntable and check the trunk lines for shape and position. Angular changes, those small kinks and bends in trunks and branches, are partly created now by pruning above buds pointed in directions sharply divergent from the main lines. These linear changes do a lot to create an impression of age. As the tree grows, it absorbs some of this fine detail. One way of keeping the detail, or at least some of it, is to exaggerate the changes in the growth lines by selecting buds that will create a zigzag growth pattern as they develop.

You can add to this in early summer by wiring the main branch lines. Remember that the wood is brittle. Seal any larger cuts and let the plant grow strongly. A lot of inner buds will be produced, adding to the bulk of foliage. When the growth has lengthened, pinch it back to develop branch contours. This applies chiefly to the minor trunk. The major trunk is allowed to maintain and extend its higher position, which is done by allowing the line to push upwards without too much lateral competition.

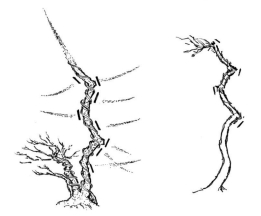

Left: the tree is wired and the branches are pruned selectively. **Right:** the trunks are cut back and re-grown several times.

Watch the wires! They will be tight in weeks. Cut them off, because if you try to uncoil the wire, you will damage the branches.

Follow this programme while you build up the two trunk forms. The lesser trunk will be developed with a cap of gnarled branches forming the canopy. The taller trunk is formed as a curved line, gnarled by abruptly straight areas. This is brought about by extending the line, wiring, pruning and re-growing the line. It is varied by how much extension time and degree of curvature is allowed between each process. This system is followed for as long as it takes the plant to grow to 60cm (2ft) high. Then the canopy is formed to echo that of the short trunk.

Those are the practical mechanics. The creation of the twin trunks is constantly scrutinized, reviewed and adjusted to keep the overall balance of the form. It will probably take about five years to complete the basic relationship. After that is achieved, you can follow the routine care suggested on page 99.

The tree after five years.

One great stumbling block as you create something like this is a natural impatience to get through it quickly so that you can enjoy your finished work. Whatever you do, do not use high nitrogen feeds to encourage fast growth because all the fine detail is lost if you do. Stick with fish emulsion and 0–10–10. This method will keep everything in scale but will take longer to achieve the magnificent 8cm (3in) trunk diameter than the faster, field-grown trunk version.

The slower version is often better because the trunk and branches have a more natural-looking taper and none of the major scarring of the heavily cut-back field tree. Of course, if you do not mind the wait while the scars heal over and mature bark forms, the fast-grown version has the initial advantage of the 'trunk in the hand'!

The final touch in the tree was the simple pot. It was about 30cm (12in) square by 10cm (4in) deep and was a matt midnight blue. I still remember the Japanese 'offering picture', which showed the silver-grey bark, the fabulous shape, the scarlet berries, the bright green moss and that blue pot!

Bonsai Re-creation

This Japanese deciduous holly was imported in 1988. It is a fine example of field development, in which the trunk has been allowed to recover and generate good secondary and tertiary extensions after the first major and subsequent styling cuts in the field. The plant was probably fully grown when it was initially cut back. This type of holly actually develops into a large shrub, so it is possible that the trunk was around 3m (10ft) high.

HEIGHT: 64cm (25in); trunk diameter 10cm (4in); AGE: quoted as 60 years but probably about 30 years.

Trunk Reconstruction The interesting thing with this example is that you can virtually read the tree's history if you check the trunk line. The trunk

At last, the tree can be transplanted into the dark blue, square pot.

The deciduous Japanese holly (Ilex serrata) in fruit.

A close-up of the base of the trunk.

was cut four times to change the direction of growth and to build taper. The first trunk pruning was probably done at 10 years or so, the second cut at 17 years and the third and fourth cuts at 22 and 26 years. This would allow enough bark healing and growing time to develop the apical area and main branch lines. Another factor that reinforces this theoretical timescale is the formation of the mature silver-grey bark, which does not appear on immature trees.

The present owner of the tree told me that he grew seedlings from the batch of berries appearing in the year of importation. These are largely male and the tree fruits regularly as a result.

The old trunk shortening zones were carefully covered with wound sealant paste, which proved to have sealed in enough moisture to have rotted each of these areas. I peeled this away and pulled out the soft, rotting wood, leaving the areas exposed to the air to dry out.

I removed some of the soil dressing of red akadama soil to expose some more roots. The wonderful dull blue glazed pot by Gordon Duffett is a perfect foil to the red berries and grey bark.

The photograph above shows the roots after the red soil had been removed. Many of the roots had actually been buried up to this point. Remember

The holly viewed from the back.

A detail of the branches.

my tip about checking for surface roots under the red soil on imported trees? Here it is in action!

There is a hybrid of deciduous Japanese holly (*Ilex serrata*) and winterberry (*Ilex verticillata*), named 'Sparkleberry', which is a deciduous, female holly that grows to 3.7m (12ft) and has brilliant red fruits, 10mm (⅜in) across. The pollinator is *Ilex serrata × I. verticillata* 'Apollo', which is a male holly. There are other female forms of *I. verticillata*, which are more compact in habit and which would be well worth trying as Shohin bonsai.

Pomegranate

The pomegranate *(Punica granatum)* is a much loved tree throughout the Mediterranean, and in California, the Spanish fondness for planting a pomegranate tree near to their houses led to their appearing in the grounds of early dwellings. Some of these old trees have now been adapted to life as bonsai, and they look very happy. The Japanese also like pomegranate and have developed many varieties with different coloured flowers.

As a bonsai the pomegranate has much to offer. The tree structure is elegant, with good branching and many fine twigs. Some cultivars have very coarse bark and some have natural twisting of the trunk. The leaves are mid- to dark green, and the brilliant orange-red, waxy flower buds and open flowers are very attractive.

There are some problems. The tree is not hardy and needs to be regarded as a greenhouse subject or, at the very least, a plant that must be kept in frost-free conditions. The branches are very brittle and need careful handling.

Containers in quiet blues, yellows and unglazed browns and greys are suitable. Pomegranates like water, so do not use pots that are too shallow. The

A close-up of a pomegranate flower.

trees suit a formal pot, but if a strongly geometric shape is used, try to soften it by choosing a muted colour but nothing too dark.

Seasonal Care

Training Styles Informal, Leaning, Semi-cascade, Cascade, Literati, Root over Rock, Tree on Rock, Twin-trunk, Raft, Root-connected, Group.

Likely Source Pomegranates are sometimes available as local nursery stock, especially the dwarf form *Punica granatum* var. *nana;* they are also available as imported Japanese bonsai stock.

Propagation The pomegranate is easily propagated from cuttings and seed or by layering and division.

Type and Description A small, deciduous, flowering and fruiting tree.

Habitat America, Asia and Europe.

Trunk Young shoots are green and flushed orange-red, maturing to buff-grey. Branches are heavily twigged. The orange-brown bark becomes deeply fissured with age.

Foliage Leaves are narrowly spear-shaped and have smooth edges. They often have a curvy appearance. Shoots are green, flushed with orange. New growth shoots are thin but vigorous in habit and soon form arching sprays of leaves.

Flowers Flowers are usually vermilion. Flower buds are terminally borne and look like inverted pears as they develop. Flowers open with a smooth, shiny outer shell and crumpled interior petals.

Fruit Depending on the variety, the red fruits produced range from golf-ball to apple size. They are shallowly segmented.

Cultivars There are many cultivars in Japan where the plant was extensively hybridized. Commonly used and available are: *P. granatum* var. *nana* – dwarf form, normally multi-stemmed, with small, red flowers and small fruit and leaves; *P. g.* 'Nejikan' – a variety with a naturally twisted trunk and coarse bark and red flowers.

Soil Two parts sand, five parts mixed composted peat and leaf mould and three parts akadama.

Potting and Repotting Never use shallow containers when potting because this tree flowers well when slightly root-bound and it needs soil capacity and a reservoir effect to support it in this condition.

Repot in mid-spring when the buds are on the move. Young trees are repotted every year. Older plants are repotted as indicated by root production, which means gently tapping the root mass free of the pot and checking for areas of soil not yet permeated with root. If there is still soil available, repotting is delayed for another season.

Water Keep damp at all times. Before mid-season, shade the tree slightly to conserve moisture. This enables the grower to monitor water without harming the tree. By keeping the pomegranate slightly dry at this period, the tree is encouraged to set flowering shoots. A lot of water at this stage will induce lush leaf shoots. After flowers appear, water is given freely for the rest of the season.

Feeding Feed when leaves swell until the flowering period, using half-strength Miracle-Gro, or a similar feed, alternately with 0–10–10 every 10 days. After the flowering period, if there are any fruit formed, recommence the feeding cycle but also feed monthly until early autumn with fish emulsion.

Trimming Older branches can be pruned in mid-season. New shoots are pinched from early summer, keeping at least two leaves on each shoot. Flower buds are produced at this period, and earlier pruning can remove them. Flowering shoots are usually shorter than leaf shoots. Do not cut flowering shoots. Remember to check as you work: flowers are carried at the terminals. Repeat trimming as necessary.

Wiring Wire in mid-season, using aluminium wire. All wood is brittle and breaks easily.

Position Place pomegranates in good light. They like sunlight, but must be kept watered. They must be protected from frost.

Pests and Diseases Essentially free trouble, pomegranates may sometimes be affected by aphids. Treat with pyrethrum or a similar insecticide.

Material Type

The pomegranate is not hard to find in garden centres, but it is most often encountered as the dwarf form *P. g.* var. *nana*. The dwarf tree is fine and makes a very nice bonsai, but what are your options is you want something bigger?

As with the deciduous holly, the best plan is probably to visit a bonsai nursery and obtain a tree that you can use as both a specimen bonsai and as a stock plant. Imported bonsai pomegranates are usually overgrown and can lose a few branches. Most bonsai nurseries still import as part of their annual shipments from Japan large numbers of the variety 'Nejikan', which has a twisted trunk. These plants are usually good for donating cuttings. Let us assume you have been to a good quality nursery and you have a bushy pomegranate. Now, where do you start?

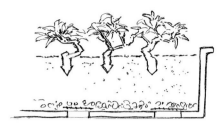

The cuttings are allowed plenty of root run.

The tools and equipment you will need and the method are described under How Bonsai are Created (see pages 16–17).

The transplanted cutting are already looking tree-like.

A very bushy and overgrown imported pomegranate bonsai. The idea is to make a Group by using the stocky branches as cuttings.

The difference between pomegranate and most other trees is you can take heavy branches of the pomegranate tree, root them and get fat little trees that are ideal for Shohin or a Group.

Starting with year 2, after the cuttings are well established as separately potted plants, you can begin styling for Group planting by assembling them in order of trunk forms. This approximate position will give you an idea of trunk shape and movement. You can even attempt some rough contouring as the plants put out their mass of shoots. Feed and water them well and they will shape up fast as little trees. Protect them over winter – they hate frost.
In year 3 you can set up the Group.

All the branches have great character.

The transplanted pomegranate 'trees' are arranged by trunk form and size in a rough grouping so that they can be grown and pruned as a unit in the establishment year.

You will need: shears, fine scissors, branch cutters, wire cutters, soil probe, soil sieve, potting soil, soil scoop, aluminium wire, turntable and prepared containers.
Season: as buds break in mid-spring.

Choose a bonsai container that is either elliptical or rectangular and about 5cm (2in) deep. Consider the size of the Group in terms of height and spread. The container looks best if it has at least 20 per cent of unoccupied space around the trunks. Another factor is that of perspective: the container needs to be broad enough to provide a sense of recession, without 'pinching the toes' of the trees.

Another 'must' is a trunk location grid. Root systems are tied to the grid, which enables the grower to site trees accurately and safely. The grid must sit in the container and support the trunks without buckling, so it needs to be made of split garden canes or 5mm (¼ in) gauge aluminium training wire. Make a mesh of 5cm (2in) squares, using finer wire or plastic cinch ties to tie off intersections. Make sure the mesh sits flat in the container.

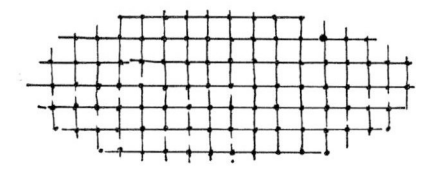

Make a grid from wire or split garden canes.

The container should have the standard plastic drainage mesh, but you will find it helpful to cover the floor of the pot with drainage netting so that there are fewer things to catch on when you are busy locating the trunks. Put plenty of tie wires up through the drainage holes and drape the ends over the pot rim so that they are kept well out the way. Add a drainage course and a bed of the suggested soil mix and you are ready.

Viewing the container from above, the Group will probably be planted around and slightly behind the main axis, and off-centre or somewhere towards the one-third position along it. Look for trunks that

are thicker than the rest and for some thinner ones, too. The heavier lines are useful for accenting clusters within the arrangement, and the finer lines can suggest distance when used towards the back.

While we are still considering the overhead view, remember that the plan of the planting will work if attention is paid to creating a nucleus of trunks, contrasted with a thin line of trunks – almost like a comma, for example.

Viewed from straight on at eye level, this arrangement provides depth through the trunks, and the simple trunk line placed at the back suggests space and distance, especially if smaller and lighter trees are used.

The lines in the Group work best if there is harmony between them. The 'trees' being raised from bonsai branches will often have a pleasing unity of form. The duller and more repetitive the branches on the donor tree, the better the present arrangement! The original tree will be better without them, too.

The height of the arrangement is worth thinking about. With this material, it is likely that most of the plants are compact, maybe 15–23cm (6–9in) tall at the most. There is nothing wrong with those proportions if you want to make a low and powerful scene, reminiscent of a coastal grove, or some far distant view perhaps. There are probably all sorts of side branches already on the trunks, left over from their previous existence, and these can be readily used. If a taller Group is planned, it may be an advantage to remove the side branches to emphasize the trunk lines.

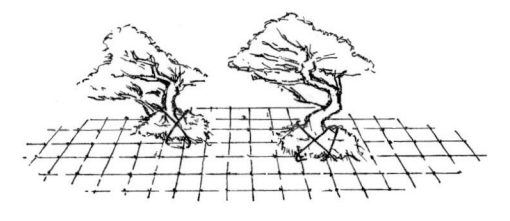

In year 2 the main trees are lightly root-pruned lightly and tied in position on the grid.

Using the grid, position the major trunks first. They will need to be planted higher so, as you remove them from the growing pots, take less of the soil depth away. Use the soil probe to unravel the roots and spread them out. Root-prune lightly, then locate and tie the trees to the grid.

The trees will stay put and this makes trying the companion trunks for line and position much easier. Choose secondary trunk lines that harmonize and plant them a little lower than the main ones. Go on adding trunks and building up the depth of the grove. Remember to leave space for the lesser trunks at the back so that they can grow, too. Preserve space around and between so that you can clearly see through the arrangement without visual conflict. That does not mean to say the trunks have to be remote from each other – you are not emulating Stonehenge.

Secondary trees are added and tied in place on the grid.

The basic arrangement is completed.

Part of the beauty of the grid is that it allows you to butt trunks hard against each other if you wish. If you want to do this, it is quite safe to remove roots to allow trunk lines to sit together.

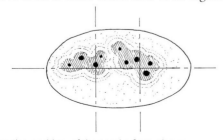

Assess the position of the trunks from above.

The initial planting does take time, but when the Group is planted and secured to the grid, simply pop the whole unit into the pot and secure the grid with the tie wires. Add more soil and spend time sifting it in and around the intermeshed roots. You

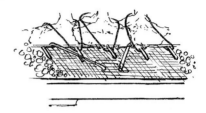

Place the grid in the pot. Drainage netting is used to carpet the pot floor from side to side. Tie wires are passed through the drainage holes. The drainage course is added and then some soil. The grid is lowered into the pot and tied in place.

If trunks are intended to fit closely together, the inner root section should be removed. The trunks are tied together and then fastened to the grid.

Carefully add soil with a scoop. Make sure the soil really fills all the crevices between the root masses.

The Group and the grid can be transferred successfully to the container. The surface soil may be contoured and mossed.

can use the soil probe to find and fix any holes. Do not tamp the soil too much. You can add moss between surfaced roots if you have made these into a feature. If you have not, you can still use the moss around the trunk clusters.

Water the Group planting in well with a fine spray and place it in a shaded spot in a plastic green-house (poly-tunnel). Aftercare is standard. As the planting settles, it will produce a mass of shoots. These should be carefully thinned and pruned to maintain negative space and to enhance branch planes.

In year 2 the Group can be wired as needed. Check that the root ties from the grid are not biting in, and cut them if necessary.

Repot in year 3, removing the grid but keeping the trunks together as a single root pad. Follow the schedule for caring for pomegranate (see page 107) and after a very short time you will have an out-standing bonsai, with a lot of character.

Bonsai Re-creation

This imported pomegranate tree, *Punica granatum* 'Neijikan', was developed from a fast-grown plant.

The twin, curved trunk line (see photographs over-leaf) is pleasing and re-creates the feeling of a wild pomegranate.

HEIGHT: 38cm (15in); trunk diameter 8cm (3in); AGE: quoted as 40 years but probably about 20 years.

Trunk Reconstruction The plant was probably raised from a multi-stemmed cutting. There is a stump of a third trunk still showing. In such a case

The field-grown tree is cut hard back. The central trunk dies back.

A pomegranate bonsai in the mist.

The pomegranate before styling. The photograph was taken in 1997.

The same pomegranate after styling, also photographed in 1997.

the rooted cutting is planted out and fed heavily. The trunk forms are typical of the upcurved growth habit of strong green growth and lend a naturalness of line to the bonsai. The shape evolved from these lines as they matured and thickened. The trunks were allowed to develop freely for a number of years and then were cut hard back. The overall height was probably reduced from about 3m (10ft).

Branch Reconstruction When the tree was exported it had only a simple frame of shortened branch spurs, covered in a mass of twigs. The effect was of a fully contoured tree, but on closer inspection

it was obviously a cosmetic exercise for export purposes. There were, in fact, no real structures or design.

Since then there has been a lot of branch growth, and the sub-branches have been developed with a convincing amount of twig growth. The method is to grow, wire and prune in the same way as described for the hawthorn (see page 89).

The imported tree after some adequate branch development.

Tight little spur branches develop, and these carry a pseudo-contour of little twigs.

Root Structure The roots are well-placed and strong. They were spread radially when the pomegranate was first planted out, and they have now matured into lines that really support the trunk base.

Quince

Most members of the quince family bear flowers in late winter and are strong and reliable year after year. They are a splendid sight when they are grown as wall shrubs, with their mainly red, cupped flowers, and when they are grown as bonsai, their almost primitive, simple branches really show off the vivid flowers.

Japanese quince (*Chaenomeles speciosa*, syn. *Cydonia japonica*) forms natural clumps, and when it is treated as a bonsai this growth habit can be used in making superb Group style plants. If you choose the right species, you can successfully make a tiny

tree from, say, a dwarf quince like C. *speciosa* 'Chojubai', or a heavy-trunked giant from a Chinese quince (*Pseudocydonia sinensis*, syn. *Chaenomeles sinensis*). Quince also look wonderful in rock-grown plantings. There are no major problems with the genus.

Container colours that work are the now-familiar dull blues, yellows and off–whites. Unglazed ware also looks very pleasing with very old material. Clumps of quince look good grown in oval containers, while the stronger growing Chinese quince looks good in a medium depth oval or rectangle.

Seasonal Care

Training Styles Japanese quince: Informal, Leaning, Semi-cascade, Cascade, Literati, Root over Rock, Tree on Rock, Twin-trunk, Raft, Root-connected, Group. Dwarf Japanese quince (*C. speciosa* 'Chojubai'): Informal, Leaning, Semi-cascade, Cascade, Tree on Rock, Raft, Root-connected, Group, Shohin. Chinese quince: Informal, Leaning, Semi-cascade, Cascade, Root over Rock, Twin-trunk, Raft, Group.

Likely Source Japanese quince: readily available as garden centre and local nursery stock; sometimes available as imported Japanese bonsai stock as the variety 'Toyonishiki'; importers do not recognize it. Dwarf Japanese quince *(C. speciosa* 'Chojubai'): sometimes available as imported Japanese bonsai; importers do not recognize it. Chinese quince: readily available as imported Japanese bonsai.

Propagation Japanese quince: very easy to propagate from cuttings or by division or by layering. Dwarf Japanese quince *(C. speciosa* 'Chojubai'): very easy to propagate from cuttings or by division. Chinese quince: very easy to propagate from cuttings and by layering; it can also be propagated from seed.

Type and Description A deciduous, flowering, fruiting shrub.

Habitat Asia, America and Europe.

Trunk Young shoots are green, maturing to buff and then to a silver grey bark. Some types of Quince are very shrubby with no clear single trunk. The Chinese quince has a strong trunk and develops exfoliating bark, leaving a patterned under-bark of green and buff, similar to that seen on plane trees.

Foliage The oval leaves are slightly toothed, bright green, and new growth is flushed red. The leaves of Chinese quinces are larger, oval and have toothed edges; they are dark green and sticky to the touch.

Flowers The flowers of Japanese quince, which are anything from white through pink, orange, red to deep scarlet, are usually 2.5cm (1in) across, cupped, with crisply curved petals.

Note: do not move this plant around too much once the flowers swell up because they easily drop.

The flowers of the Chinese quince are quite different: they are lipstick pink in bud, the petals are narrower and open almost flat. The flowers then turn white or pale pink.

Fruit Fruits of Japanese quince are usually about golf-ball size. They are green, turning to a golden-yellow, and are often fragrant. The fruits of the Chinese quince reach apple size and are very fragrant.

Cultivars There are a lot of cultivars to choose from; I have included just some of the best. There are some dwarf quince species that are worth trying, but these do need a little more care. Dwarf quince: *Chaenomeles japonica* var. *alpina* – bright orange flowers; *C. j.* 'Chojubai' – there are red- and white-flowered forms. Flowering quince: *Chaenomeles japonica* – orange-flame flowers, a vigorous form. The following varieties are strong plants: *Chaenomeles speciosa* 'Brilliant' – scarlet flowers; *C. s.* 'Cardinalis' – bright red, double flowers; *C. s.* 'Moerloosei' – pink and white flowers; *C. s.* 'Nivalis' – white flowers; *C. s.* 'Toyonishiki' – white, pink, red, solid and threaded coloured petals, recalling a Satsuki azalea; *C. s.* 'Versicolor Lutescens'. – cream-yellow, flushed pink; *C. × superba* 'Pink Lady' – rose pink flowers.

Soil Two parts sand, five parts mixed composted peat and leaf mould and three parts akadama.

Potting and Repotting Quince has weak roots and is, for this reason, usually better repotted in early to mid-autumn, when it is less likely to pick up soil-borne disease.

Water Keep well watered and spray the leaves except during the flowering season.

Feeding Feed every 10 days from when the leaves appear until mid-autumn with 0–10–10 and fish emulsion. Do not feed during the flowering period. Resume feeding Chinese quince when the fruit swells. Dose the tree once each year with Trace Element Frit.

Trimming New growth is allowed to grow and thicken up before it is tip-pruned in late spring or early summer. This induces a lot of budding and the secondary shoots are again allowed to grow freely. Secondary growth is shortened back in early winter, when the fatter flower buds can be distinguished from the leaf buds. Shoots are shortened back adjacent to a cluster of flower buds. As the tree flowers it looks as if the branch tips are erupting colour. When old branches are pruned, it is better to shorten them first, making it a two-season operation because quince can suffer from die-back if heavy branches are lopped off.

Wiring Wire quince in early summer. Use aluminium wire. Quince is very brittle. Remember that you are going to cut away a lot of terminal growth, so concentrate on shaping the initial few centimetres of new growth. Chinese quince are wired before bud break, and new shoots are wired in early summer.

Position Place in good light but do not let quince get too hot. Protect plants from hard frost.

Pests and Diseases Aphids, borers and nematodes can be a problem. Aphids can be treated with a mild insecticide. Borers are best tackled with systemic insecticides and a little poured directly into the holes is a good method. Nematodes are best treated by cutting away the affected parts and treating with sulphur spray.

The flowers of C. speciosa 'Nivalis'.

Japanese flowering quince, Chaenomeles japonica 'Choujubai'.

A close-up of the flowers of variety *C. speciosa* 'Toyonishiki'.

Bonsai Re-creation

There is more than one clone of this variety of Japanese flowering quince, *Chaeonomeles speciosa* 'Toyonishiki'. This particular plant bears red, red and white, and white flowers simultaneously. It was imported in 1988 and is a good example of a clump bonsai. The clustered trunk lines are well formed and there will many buds sprouting from the trunk if more lines are wanted.

HEIGHT: 40cm (16in); triple trunks, total diameter at base: 8cm (3in); AGE: approximately 10 years.

Trunk Reconstruction The plant was probably raised from a division. It is easy to make a 'stool bed' with this species by simply earthing up the base of plants in open growth. This encourages roots and more suckers to form, and stool beds can yield many plants in a season or two.

At this stage, trunks and branches need further development by the grow-and-cut method, but they

Japanese flowering quince, *Chaenomeles speciosa* 'Toyonishiki'.

A cluster Group of Japanese flowering quince was created by division. An old garden plant was transplanted.

After five years the plant is on the way.

Bonsai Re-creation

This Japanese flowering quince, *Chaenomeles × superba* 'Pink Lady', was raised from a layering taken from a garden plant by Peggy Kemp. She made a very good choice of trunk section, including some very fine branches in with the trunk.

HEIGHT: 38cm (15in); spread: 60cm (24in): trunk diameter 5cm (2in); AGE: 30 years.

Assess the plant at eye level.

will soon become very pleasing. The lines need extra thickness and denser growth.

The pot, a medium quality Japanese pot, is not unpleasant, but think what Gordon could do for this tree!

Prune the desired section.

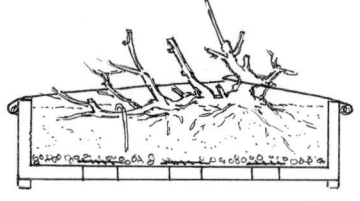

The division is transferred to a growing box. Side branches are pegged down to root and add width.

A close-up of the buds of *C.* x *superba* 'Pink Lady'.

Japanese flowering quince, *Chaenomeles* x *superba* 'Pink Lady'.

I continued her design, but used a downswept planting angle because it cried out to be a Semi-cascade, but I kept the lines simple, following the grow-and-cut method. This echoes the staccato movements already in the primary branches. The present owner of the Quince is happy to continue the work and, like me, he likes the unusual round Japanese pot. The glaze is 'hare's foot' Chun in a dull blue, which tones with the deep pink-red cupped flowers.

It is interesting how, because the plant has remained in a pot, it remains dainty in feeling despite being 30 years old. Planted out it would have been huge.

The flowers of *C.* x *superba* 'Pink Lady'.

The fat flower buds.

Wisteria

The wisteria is a much-loved plant, and the cascading racemes of flowers often seen on old wall vines are staggeringly beautiful.

It is simple to grow as bonsai if you follow the notes included here. Most people use too large a container and, when this is combined with too frequent and too lush a soil change, the plant happily grows away without a flower in sight. That is probably why in Britain at least, wisteria is not popular as bonsai. When treated as suggested, however, the plant flowers well and is a joy.

Containers in greens, blues, off-white and light greys are all pretty with this species. By all means try wisteria as a cascade bonsai – it follows the natural form – but if you use a deep Cascade pot to carefully balance the design, do not give the roots too much room.

Seasonal Care

Training Styles Leaning, Semi-cascade, Cascade, Root over Rock.

Likely Source Wisterias are readily available as local and specialist nursery stock, and as imported Japanese bonsai.

Propagation Wisteria is easily propagated by layering, and it is not too difficult from cuttings and by division or grafts. It is slow from seed.

Type and Description A deciduous, flowering vine.

Habitat China, Japan.

Trunk Young growth is green and matures to buff. The bark thickens with age to a silver-brown.

Foliage On the Japanese wisteria *(Wisteria floribunda)* growth extends, in a clockwise direction, before the flowers, as vine-like tendrils produce compound leaves with many dark green leaflets. On the Chinese wisteria *(Wisteria sinensis)* growth extends after the flowers, in a counter-clockwise direction.

Flowers The violet-blue or bluish-purple, fragrant flowers of Japanese wisteria are carried in racemes from 13–30cm (5–12in) long. Flowers open successively from the base of the raceme downwards. The fragrant flowers of the Chinese wisteria are mauve or deep lilac and borne in racemes 20–30cm (8–12in) long. Flowers open simultaneously.

Fruit These are seed pods about 10cm (4in) long. They are light brown and are velvety to the touch.

Cultivars Japanese wisteria: *W. floribunda* 'Alba' – white flowers in racemes 44–60cm (18–24in) long; *W. f.* 'Rosea' ('Honko') – rose-pink flowers, tipped with purple, in racemes 50cm (20in) or more long; *W. × formosa* 'Issai' ('Domino') – lilac-blue flowers in racemes 15–25cm (6–10in) long. Chinese wisteria: *W. sinensis* 'Alba' – white flowers in racemes 30cm (12in) long; *W. s.* 'Black Dragon' – dark purple, double flowers; *W. s.* 'Plena' – lilac, double flowers.

Soil Two parts sand, five parts composted peat, four parts akadama and one part good compost create the heavy soil wisteria prefer.

Potting and Repotting Use deep pots. Repot every five years or so, after the flowering period. The reason for the long delay is that potted wisteria bloom well if they are stressed. The deep pots enable the plants to function, even when they are rootbound, and they also complement the cascading flowers.

Wash and soak away the old soil. Cut only the dead and darker looking roots, trimming back to live white tissue. Keep the fine roots and coil long roots around the pot rather than cutting them. Do

Fully opened flowers.

not use a coarse, lower drainage soil because the roots will locate this and grow vigorously, and the plant will not flower.

Water Wisteria love water, but more than that, as part of the intentional stress treatment, they are placed in water during the growing season. The water stifles the lower roots of oxygen and slows down the growth of roots and branches. The plant is threatened and flowers to reproduce itself. Keeping it in water with enough feed, and with the upper part of the soil/root mass clear of the water to allow the air exchange to take place, keeps the plant happy and induces flowering.

Stand the plant in water so that 25 per cent of the pot is immersed. Keep the plant in the water container from one month after flowering (in the repotting year) until early autumn. In an ordinary

Some of the shoots can also be wired. If the tree is pruned like this for a few years, it will soon develop a good shape.

New growth on older plants is trimmed back, keeping two or three compound leaves. The first trimming is done right after flowering and repeated about a month later. Older branches can be pruned at repotting time. Thin any new inner leaf buds that are not wanted for shape improvement.

Wiring Wire shortly after the flowering period. Use aluminium wire. Wisterias are very brittle, and older wood is best shaped with pruning.

Position Wisterias like good light, but do not let them get too much hot sun. They can take a little frost, but it may be better to keep them frost free.

Pests and Diseases Wisterias are largely trouble free. If scale insects are a problem, treat with a mild insecticide.

Material Type

One of the nicest things you can do in raising wisteria bonsai is to go pick a section on an old wall shrub and induce it to root by layering.

For the tools you will need and the method follow the suggested layering procedure on page 20. The great thing about layering is that you can really choose the shape you want. Imagine a classic Semi-cascade wisteria with the bonus of an old and gnarled trunk thrown in! That is layering!

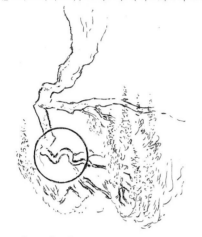

A Cascade wisteria is developed by air layering. First, find a suitable section.

year keep it submerged from flowering onwards. Change the water occasionally.

Feeding From bud swelling to flowering feed with 0-10-10, fish emulsion and half-strength Miracle-Gro. Alternate the feeds every 10 days. Do not feed during flowering, but afterwards feed until autumn, alternating the three feeds. You can also add feed to the water in the standing container. This will keep the foliage green. Dose with Trace Element Frit once a year.

Trimming Young plants with an immature, vine-like shape are fed and watered heavily to encourage strong growth and are then pinched back in mid-season. The shoots are cut back to two or three leaves. They will sprout again, shoot out and these secondary shoots are shortened again. This builds a system of short, woody and characterful branches.

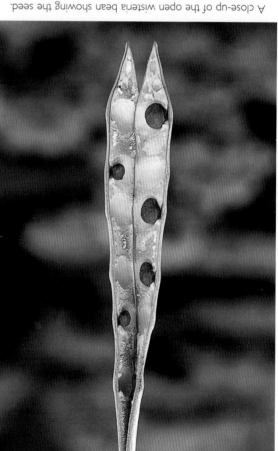

A close-up of the open wisteria bean showing the seed.

Left; Ring the bark. **Right;** Peel the bark away.

Add rooting hormone.

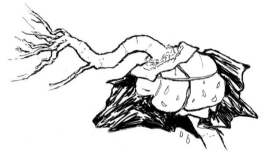

Wrap sphagnum moss, clear and black plastic around the peeled section.

Styling can begin as soon as your layering feels firm in the pot. This is usually about three years after layering, including a safety margin. 'Styling' is, in fact, too rigid a word for the process involved – it is much more a question of responding to the shape of the trunk.

The rooted layer is tied into the container at an angle. Use a pressure pad to cushion the trunk.

Most trees in the Semi-cascade shape work with a simple platform of spur branches on the end of the arching trunk. With a layered tree, it is likely that you will have a really unpredictable shape, and one that will set your tree apart – even make it great!

Throughout, my opinion has been that the trunk represents the sculptural core of the design. If you think of the shape as being in tune with that central theme, that is it! The trunk sets the tone for the whole thing. If it is rippled, echo that shape as you shape the branches. If it is gnarled, add something of that.

The practical mechanics of shaping such a tree begin with setting it at the right angle. Earlier, I mentioned the idea of using bean bags to prop a tree (see page 30), and this is a useful approach to adopt at this point. You need to assess 'where and how', and with a Semi-cascade much of the design is to do with main angles. You need to initiate a strong trunk line and a jutting frame of branches, so that the flowers drop their racemes into a believable space.

It is a good idea to rest the wisteria the day before exercising it by not watering, as this relaxes the wood somewhat and makes it easier to wire.

Sometimes, sitting the existing pot sideways and halfway into the top of a smaller pot, will give you a good working angle. You can still use the bean bags to pack and prop the main pot.

Prop up the pot to aid in styling.

After wiring the branches work with the trunk form.

Now the trunk is lowered and the freely grown branches are ready for shaping. What should you do first?

Check the branches for flexibility. If they flex, you can wire them gently and not too tightly and bend them to spread and extend the elegance of the curved trunk. Remember the 'finger clamp' technique (see page 13). It will work, even on those creaky branches, provided that you work slowly and squeeze as you bend.

After about five years the tree is potted in a deep container and displayed on a tall stand fashioned from a tree root. An old currant bush could be used to produce such a base.

With the main lines successfully trained, you can select side limbs and shorten those. Usually there is not much to do beyond the wiring and branch shortening.

Repot at the new angle. Do not take much root off and do not use too big a pot. Give it a year off following the styling, making sure it is root-bound and well watered and fed, and flowers will not be far behind. Enjoy your Wisteria. I am sure it will not be the last one you do.

Bonsai Re-creation

This imposing Chinese wisteria *(W. sinensis)* was purchased as a nursery seedling approximately 12mm (½ in) thick in 1972. The owner and trainer, John Lee, generously shared the training programme that he followed.

HEIGHT: 69cm (27in); trunk diameter 15cm (6in); AGE: approximately 27 years.

The wisteria in 1993, photographed after the carving session.

Trunk Reconstruction In 1972 the seedling was initially planted against a screen wall.

In October 1977, after five years of free growth, the wisteria was pruned back and transplanted to another property, where it was planted centrally next to a south-facing wall, 6.1m (20ft) wide. It was allowed to grow out to the width of the wall until 1990, allowing it 13 years of extended growth.

In February 1990 it was transplanted to an open, sunny position in the garden. The roots and branches were pruned back to the span of 1–1.2m (3–4ft). In March 1993 it was transplanted to a large PVC pot. John brought the tree to one of my work-shops in May 1993, and we worked on carving the upper portion of the trunk to echo the scarred opening of the bark in the lower part. I took great care not to disturb the plant too much. The photograph above shows it after we had carved it. Notice how tentative the carving has been, but the tree can easily accept this degree of change.

I suggested that the turquoise glaze developed by Dan Barton, if used on a simple, deepish, oval pot, would do great things for the emerging tree image. John agreed and here is the result. The tree–pot union is very successful. The blue-green

A close-up of the trunk.

glaze is dark on the wall of the pot where the darker body colour comes through, then concentrates in the strip of lighter intense colour at the base. The combination is spectacular.

Branch Reconstruction The drawings supplied by John of growth at the end 1996 indicate the results of his grow-and-cut methods. He has built some very interesting and diverse branches in the short period of three years! Compare the 1993 version.

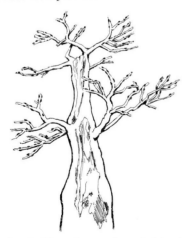

All the drawings in this section are from sketches by John and show the developing structure very well. The trunk terminal has been shortened, and the pruning stumps visible in the 1993 photograph have been removed.

John summarized his technique as follows. Over the years, summer growth is reduced back to five nodes (leaf joints). Each February, growth is shortened to two nodes if there is no frost about. Late in each autumn he gives bonemeal as a surface feed. In summer generous amounts of water are given and, since the wisteria has been potted, it has stood in a shallow tray of water filled daily throughout the summer months. He feeds liberally with Phostrogen, a water-soluble powder with an analysis of 10–10–27.

A detail showing how the pruning works and the position of the sample branch.

Left: A closer detail showing how pruning triggers budding. **Centre and right:** A fine detail of an emerging bud and the previous season's leaf joint.

You will notice that this parallels the cultural data in Seasonal Care (pages 119–21), apart from the late winter pruning. Other skilled growers practise this technique on some deciduous trees with great success. They feel the advantages are that the very worst of the bad weather is largely past and the sacrificed sections have nurtured the plant with no cuts for the worst winter frosts to worry.

The potted tree in full flower, photographed in spring 1997.

Glossary

akadama Japanese red subsoil.

aphids Greenfly.

basal shoots Strong shoots appearing from low on the trunk or as root suckers.

Bordeaux mixture A mildew treatment solution containing copper sulphate.

borers Insects that tunnel into the trunks. Treat with pyrethrum injected into the holes.

branch/trunk echo Taking the trunk shape as the theme for branch shaping.

bud blast Brown discoloration of buds. Remove dark buds and treat with Bordeaux mixture.

bud break As the first new green splits the bud cases.

Cascade Bonsai form where the trunk descends below the base of the pot.

celadon green A soft jade green glaze developed by the Chinese.

cluster group A tightly knit arrangement of trunks often in a ring.

dappled shade Shifting overhead shade like sunlight in a wood.

deadhead Removing spent flowers before they set seed.

deciduous Trees that shed their leaves each autumn.

Driftwood Bonsai form featuring silvered, exposed wood.

evergreen Trees that hold their leaves.

exfoliating Bark that comes off in scales or layers.

fast grow method Bonsai developed in free growth with copious feeding.

finger clamp technique Using hands together to squeeze wired areas where wood is brittle.

fish emulsion Mild fertilizer of around 5–2–2, used to nourish but not push growth.

gall Blister-like swellings appearing on azaleas. Treat by cutting away damage. Isolate infected plants.

gouache Water-colour paint with an opaque base.

goyo matsu Japanese five-needle pine.

grid Mesh used for locating plants when assembling a Group.

Informal Upright bonsai form where the trunk is shaped into soft curves.

jin Japanese term for silvered, dead branch.

Kiyonal A greenish, Japanese tree wound sealant. Dries dark.

lac balsam A greyish, German tree wound sealant. Dries grey.

Literati bonsai form derived from simplified brush paintings of trees.

longhorn beetle A black beetle spotted with white.

mame A form of small bonsai often 10–15cm (4–6in).

margined Flower petal is edged.

Miracid A fertilizer formulated for acid-loving plants like azaleas. High in nitrogen.

Miracle-Gro Similar fertilizer formulated for general use.

Nagoya City in southern Japan.

negative space The shapes created between the 'positives' of branch and trunk outlines.

nematode Eelworms. The types affecting quince causes root nodules. Treat with sulphur.

0–10–10 Fertilizer with that analysis, used for flower and fruit production.

pre-emergent Before leaf break.

pyrethrum An environmentally safe insecticide.

racemes Long streaming flower cluster. Flowers attached to the central stem.

Raft Bonsai form with recumbent trunk and branches as trees.

Root-connected Bonsai form with root suckers as trunks connected through the roots.

Root over rock Bonsai form where the tree grows astride a rock.

scion The top section of the graft. The piece to be propagated

Semi-cascade Bonsai form where the trunk descends to around the base of the pot or above.

shari Japanese term for silvered, exposed trunk section.

Shohin Japanese term for a small bonsai up to 30cm (12in).

stock plant A donor plant used for providing cutting material.

stratify Layered seeds stored in damp sand to induce good germination.

suiban Decorative pot without holes for displaying plants attached solely to the rock.

Superthrive A concentrated vitamin B1 solution used in transplanting.

taper Trunk form that gradually thins as it rises.

taproot The main anchor root sent down by a tree.

TEF Trace Element Frit

tendrils Curling growth.

terminals Main growth tips.

threaded Dotted lines of petal colour.

Twin-trunk Bonsai form with two related trunk lines.

understock The lower portion of the graft. A rooted plant used as a host for the scion.

uro Japanese term for decorative trunk hollow.

volck An environmentally safe insecticide. An emulsion spray

wound compound A sealing paste, often grey to match the bark.

zoned Inner portions of the petals are coloured.

Index